PRAISE FOR
TEACH for ATTENTION!

"This book is witty and spot on, perfect for the busy yet thoughtful teacher who needs effective strategies to engage that struggling K–8 student with attentional issues. If this book is in your hands, you'll realize that Ezra's tool belt is theoretically grounded, based on real-life vignettes, and readily applicable. Pick and choose or read straight through. You'll easily access creative approaches that will effortlessly make a real difference in your classroom."
—**Marcy Dann, M.A.,** board certified educational therapist

"Ezra Werb's unique ability to make analogies from our adult lives to our students' lives are what make this groundbreaking book a must read for all teachers."
—**Christine Offutt,** education specialist, Mission Hills, CA

"*Teach for Attention!* is a superb read for K–8 educators of all experience levels. As a seasoned resource specialist, Ezra reminds us of the effective tools that are readily available within our reach outside of the usual choices, preferential seating, and mini breaks for our students. His frankness about speed bumps includes relatable situations while offering genuine tested solutions through various anecdotes. Furthermore, his inclusion of tech tools to help truncate and/or facilitate student work is veritably handy. This is an essential book that all educators can refer to time and again to help the kids who struggle in academic settings."
—**Valerie Sun, Ed.D.,** EmpowerED Consulting

"With humor and great intellect, Ezra Werb has woven together a book that helps teachers, parents, and educators better understand students with attention challenges. His book is fun to read, offers different points of view, and contains concrete do's and don'ts that can easily be implemented."

—**Michelle Podemski,** third-grade teacher, Los Angeles, CA

"This book on how to promote kids' attention in learning is filled with practical and simple strategies based on what we know about the ADHD learner. Ezra's approach is positive and reflects a deep understanding that students' interests, talents, and styles provide the best cues to engagement. My favorite chapters are on finding and incorporating students' interests and employing strategies that allow movement. Using case studies and guest speakers in each chapter makes the reading both enjoyable and accessible. I highly recommend this book to everyone who cares about student engagement and enjoyment in learning."

—**Susan Baum, Ph.D.,** author of *To Be Gifted and Learning Disabled* and director of the 2e Center at Bridges Academy

TEACH for ATTENTION!

A Tool Belt of Strategies for Engaging Students with Attention Challenges

Ezra Werb, M.Ed.

free spirit
PUBLISHING®

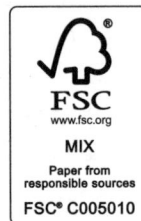

Library of Congress Cataloging-in-Publication Data
Names: Werb, Ezra, author.
Title: Teach for attention! : a tool belt of strategies for engaging students with attention challenges / Ezra Werb, M.Ed.
Description: Minneapolis, MN : Free Spirit Publishing Inc., [2019] | Includes bibliographical references and index.
Identifiers: LCCN 2018039316 (print) | LCCN 2018061651 (ebook) | ISBN 9781631983207 (Web PDF) | ISBN 9781631983214 (ePub) | ISBN 9781631983191 (pbk.) | ISBN 1631983199 (pbk.)
Subjects: LCSH: Attention-deficit-disordered children—Education (Elementary) | Learning disabled children—Education (Elementary)
Classification: LCC LC4713.2 (ebook) | LCC LC4713.2 .W37 2019 (print) | DDC 371.94—dc23
LC record available at https://lccn.loc.gov/2018039316

Edited by Eric Braun
Cover and interior design by Shannon Pourciau
Illustrated by Richard Watson

10 9 8 7 6 5 4 3 2 1
Printed in the United States of America

Free Spirit Publishing Inc.
6325 Sandburg Road, Suite 100
Minneapolis, MN 55427-3674
(612) 338-2068
help4kids@freespirit.com
www.freespirit.com

FSC
www.fsc.org
MIX
Paper from
responsible sources
FSC® C005010

Dedication

To Mom and Dad, the two best teachers I've ever known

Acknowledgments

Thanks to Eric Braun, for your editorial wisdom and fantastic ideas, and for helping this book reach its potential.

Thanks to all the creative people at Free Spirit, especially Brian Farrey-Latz, Marjorie Lisovskis, and Judy Galbraith.

Thanks to all my mentors in special education, including Marcy Dann, Nicole Messuri, and Jolie Berman. You all have helped shape my career and develop my knowledge in this field.

Thanks to all my "guest speakers": Laura Bahr, Mary McInerney, Giacomo Delgado, Chris Wiebe, Don Rice, Brian Julian, and Marcie Gilbert. Your essays add so much to this book.

Thanks to Dalia Margolis, for being such a wonderful collaborator, and to Shawn Patrick, who first showed me the importance of what we do.

Last but not least, thanks to my sweetheart, Laura, for your love and support every step of the way.

Without any of the people mentioned above, this book wouldn't have been possible.

CONTENTS

CHAPTER 3
Let Out the Fizz: How to Include Effective Fidgeting and Movement in Class 60

CHAPTER 4
Send Them in the Write Direction: How to Promote Writing Production 87

CHAPTER 5
Make a Long Story *Feel* Short: How to Engage Students in the Reading Process 112

CHAPTER 6
Teach in High Definition: How to Make Things Clear Visually 137

CHAPTER 7
Adjust Their Mirror: How to Encourage
Self-Awareness and Self-Management 162

Set the Stage to Get Engaged

It's three o'clock, and I didn't think I was going to make it.

The bell has rung, and the students are out the door. Sweet relief. All I want to do now is get in my car, throw on some *Hamilton*, and beat the traffic home. Oh wait, I almost forgot. It's Tuesday. We have our weekly after-school teachers' meeting.

I consider pulling the fire alarm.

Using better judgment, I end up sitting in the library on one of those stiff, plastic chairs while my school's technology specialist tells me how to properly input my progress reports into the new, very expensive, and very complicated online system. I know this is important, but I'd give anything at this moment to be home, relaxing on the couch or hanging out with my family and friends or prepping dinner.

Getting hungry now. Hmm, which frozen Indian meal to make tonight, the chicken masala or the lentils?

I know I should be paying attention to the tech specialist. Progress reports are really important. The parents are going to scrutinize them like tax returns. I'll have to make sure they're written perfectly.

Suddenly I'm fidgeting. Playing a light but steady drum rhythm with my pencil.

Wait, what did the tech guy just say about saving to the cloud? The reports are due Friday? I haven't even started! Oh man, I'm gonna have to write them at home. Homework is the worst.

I check the clock.

It's 4:15! I'm exhausted. No more gas in the tank. My head is so heavy, I can barely keep it propped up. I must look like a broken marionette. I really should be more awake. More engaged. Paying attention.

But sometimes, it's just really difficult.

It's difficult to sit in a room and sustain my attention on someone talking for longer than five minutes, especially when I have things I'd rather be doing, when I'm tired, when I'm hungry, when I'm fidgety, when all I want to do is jailbreak this place and escape to home.

I don't blame the tech specialist or my administrators. They're doing their best. I wouldn't want to be in their shoes, trying to teach me something at this moment.

Thank goodness this is only once a week for an hour.

And that's when it hits me.

My students with attention challenges experience this every day. They have to be in meetings for five hours a day, five days a week, thirty-six weeks a year! And *I'm* the one who is trying to engage *them*.

Sustaining engagement can be stressful for both the teacher and students.

The Challenge of Engagement

In 2016, it was estimated that 8.4 percent of US children ages two to seventeen had an ADHD diagnosis—about 5.4 million kids.[1] This is a staggering statistic that indicates a very high probability that you have at least one diagnosed student in your class, if not more. This is not counting students who are showing clear signs of attention challenges but who are not diagnosed.

We see the impact of this in our schools, with about 30 percent of students with an ADHD diagnosis failing classes and/or repeating grades. Many of these students don't make it to the end of high school, since 35 percent of diagnosed children drop out at some point.[2] These students are falling through the cracks of our educational system, and it all starts with their engagement. If students are not mentally connected to the material, the teacher, or the classroom, they are going to have an extremely difficult time performing academic tasks or learning new information that is even the least complex. Their low self-confidence will grow increasingly lower until they simply give up.

And then there are the rest of your students. Maybe they're not showing significant signs of attention difficulties, but you might notice a few students that seem a bit distracted. That one girl who seems to check out mentally when writing projects are assigned. Or that boy who is obsessed with playing a full air guitar routine with his pencil during math. Some kids simply don't connect with certain material. Other kids might not be engaged because of social or emotional struggles or because something may be happening in their home. All kids are going to have difficulty focusing at some point during the day.

But it isn't always clear how to engage students with attention challenges. Compare this to other learning issues. When a student has dyslexia or a severe language comprehension issue, it's a bit easier for teachers to wrap their heads around the situation. For example, a teacher knows that phonics and fluency support are the standard interventions for a reading issue. I'm not saying it's easy, but at least we have a roadmap. By comparison, students with attention challenges have a broad range of symptoms that cover all sorts of different areas of academic performance. When it comes to engaging students with attention issues, there is no primary solution.

So, what can we do? How do we support students in our classrooms who struggle with attention challenges?

Teaching for Attention—An Origin Story

In my thirteen years of supporting struggling students, my experiences have been diverse. I began my career doing behavior intervention with students on the autism spectrum as well as students with ADHD, helping them learn in typical classrooms and integrate socially with their peers. I then earned my special education credentials and worked as a resource specialist teacher in low-income neighborhoods of the Los Angeles Unified School District, supporting students with dyslexia, language comprehension issues, high-functioning autism, and ADHD.

In my experience, it's extremely tough to connect students with attention challenges to academic material, both in classrooms and in one-to-one settings. Like you, perhaps, I searched for strategies online and in ADHD resource books. I found many good, common sense, researched ideas: Give frequent breaks. Shorten assignments. Allow extra time for quizzes and tests. Show videos when possible. Give preferred seating. Offer choices. Repeat important information. Provide visual and verbal cues. Use positive behavior support.

I certainly use these basic supports and refer to them in this book. However, what I found time and time again was that they weren't enough. They helped in the moment but failed to result in long-term gains in engagement.

It wasn't until I earned my master's in educational therapy that I started to fully understand the implications of attention challenges on the academic lives of students and on their self-confidence. I learned to change my perspective from seeing these students as a collective group needing a strict, uniform set of supports to applying one of the principles of my educational therapy program: that every student has his or her own unique set of challenges and, more importantly, each has a unique profile of strengths and interests you can leverage to help improve his or her weaker skills.

> My mission was to focus on what these students *could* do. I began to assemble a tool belt of strategies that would build off students' strengths and make students feel confident.

As I provided academic support in typical classrooms and also conducted educational therapy sessions with students after school, my mission was to focus on what these students *could* do. I began to assemble a tool belt of strategies and supports that would build off of every student's strengths and engage each individual on a level that made that student feel confident.

If that sounds like it would take a lot of time, it did. But that doesn't mean it has to take a lot of time for you. That's what this book is for. These pages catalog all the different ways I've tried and succeeded (well, *mostly* succeeded) to engage my students—the "tools of engagement" in my tool belt—including how to harness students' interests and strengths, use technology effectively, make reading tasks feel manageable, integrate physical activity, and reinforce self-management, among many others.

In my various teaching roles, I've used all my studies, training, research, and creativity, and have tried every idea under the sun to capture students' attention. Some have worked. Some have failed.

Miserably. *Teach for Attention!* is the culmination of those efforts; I wrote it to help you learn from those successes and failures because I believe engaging kids—especially kids with attention challenges—is one of the most important things teachers can do in our highly distracting world.

Who Is This Book For?

This book is primarily for K–8 classroom teachers—or teachers of any sort, really—who want to increase their students' engagement. These strategies will help you whether you teach in a general classroom or specialize in reading, language arts, math, science, Spanish, or any other special subject. None of them require you to be an actor or a comedian or have a talent for silly voices—this book is not about putting on a show to be more engaging (of course, if you are a performer, you should definitely use that!). My tool belt has tools anyone can use without having to change your personality or style.

The *Teach for Attention!* strategies will also be helpful for specialists outside the classroom who support students with attention challenges, whether you're a tutor, educational therapist, speech therapist, occupational therapist, or in another role. Anyone who provides one-on-one support knows that even in calm, well-structured environments, it can still be extremely difficult to engage a student with your material.

Parents, too, may find ideas in this book that they can apply at home to help with the homework process.

And for the students, educators can use these strategies to help reach all those students discussed earlier—including those who are just having a tough time connecting *today* or those who struggle with a certain subject. But the students who will benefit the most are the ones with ADHD and related attention challenges.

An important point must be made here. Your students with attention deficits may also have concurrent learning and developmental challenges, including dyslexia, dysgraphia, language processing, dyscalculia, auditory or visual processing, spectrum disorders, anxiety disorders, executive function deficits, or serious behavioral challenges. Along with any of these, they may also be cognitively gifted and considered twice-exceptional; sometimes a student's cognitive gifts may result in less engagement because the student doesn't feel intellectually stimulated.

With some students, it can be extremely difficult to determine where an attention issue stops and where another deficit begins. If we suspect a student may have a concurrent cognitive or developmental issue, we as teachers have to be vocal about it. Student success teams should meet with parents and discuss what supplemental supports a student

> The strategies target students' confidence, anxiety, interest, self-awareness, sensory needs, and mental energy so students are more likely to engage with your lessons, no matter the subject.

might need: It could be a phonics program, a specialized math tutor after school, or an educational therapist to lower a student's anxiety about writing. A psychologist might also be brought in to conduct assessments and generate a cognitive profile for the student.

To be clear, my tool belt of strategies focuses on the components of attention, and the strategies are designed to be applied simply and with little preparation. In other words, they don't target specific academic muscles in the same way that a supplemental reading or writing program would, and they do not eliminate the need to deal with those other challenges. What the strategies do is target things like students' confidence, anxiety, interest, self-awareness, sensory needs, and mental energy so that students are more likely to engage with your lessons and projects, no matter the subject.

Attention and Executive Functions: The Basics

To better understand the strategies in this book and, therefore, better employ them, it's helpful to have a basic grasp of how attention and executive functions work. The *Diagnostic and Statistical Manual of Mental Disorders (DSM-5)* divides the symptoms for attention deficit hyperactivity disorder (ADHD) into two categories—inattention and hyperactivity/impulsivity—and lists the specific behaviors that correspond to each. Inattentive type is characterized by distraction and lack of focus, while students with hyperactive/impulsive type are the ones who seem energized and always on the go. Students may be diagnosed with the inattentive type, the hyperactive/impulsive type, or both, depending on their symptoms and if the symptoms appear in multiple environments.

Our attention components, as listed in the *DSM-5*, are affected greatly by our executive functions. Executive functions are how we manage ourselves and our cognitive resources in order to complete tasks and achieve goals. We're not necessarily conscious of most of these functions—like managing time, modulating mental energy, pacing ourselves, controlling impulses, switching focus, and planning ahead, just to name a few—but they are in constant use in our daily lives.

Though these functions are vast and complicated, for our purposes, we can organize them into two basic categories: our *input* abilities and our *production* (output) abilities. If students are having difficulties with input abilities, they struggle to absorb and understand material presented to them. In the classroom, that can look like this:

- appearing more interested in seemingly small stimuli around the room
- unable to stop playing with utensils at seat (rulers, pencils, sharpeners, and so on)
- asking questions about things from ten minutes ago
- unable to repeat information or directions just given
- difficulty connecting new information to what's already been taught
- seeming to be generally lost

These all are related to our ability to input information and sensory stimuli from the environment.

Then there are attention-related functions that affect our production—that is, our ability to transmit information from inside of us out to the world. Issues with work production often look like this:

- slow work production, not finishing work
- difficulty starting projects
- disorganized desks and folders
- drawing unrelated pictures on worksheets instead of working
- impulsive talking and calling out
- impulsive body movement

To help us relate to our students, consider how we all have strengths and weaknesses in these areas. For example, I consider myself a writer, and yet I have to take breaks every ten minutes when I'm writing. I have to stand up. Stretch. Walk around. Get something to eat. Send a text. Watch a stupid video of a parrot who can sing like Neil Diamond.

The takeaway is that I can produce writing, but mental energy breaks are a key part in making that happen. If I were forced to sit and produce on command without the freedom to stand up, walk around, and do something stimulating other than writing, it would be incredibly frustrating for me. And I don't have significant attention issues. This helps me realize that many of our students with ADHD may experience something similar, only much more severely, when called upon to produce work. If I can relate to a student's challenges and frustrations, it may be easier for me to find the right support.

Consider your own production abilities:

- Can you do your taxes in one sitting or do you have to take lots of breaks? Perhaps breaks are crucial for you to sustain mental energy over a long period of time.
- Do you wash dishes right away or leave them in the sink for days? Maybe you tend to avoid tasks because you perceive them as too taxing in the moment or just not much fun.
- Do you send emails and texts impulsively without really thinking about your intended meaning? You may struggle with self-editing.
- Do you obsess about paying your bills on time while your bedroom is a total disaster area? Maybe you have difficulty monitoring how much of your mental energy to put into certain tasks.
- Can you stop yourself from talking during a meeting? It may be that when you have something to say, you just have to get it out or you feel like you'll burst.

Let's talk about input abilities. Sometimes, I mentally zone out while I'm driving. I'll be cruising down the 101 freeway, thinking about the season finale of the show I just binge-watched and how disappointing it was, but I'm so invested now that of course I'm going to watch the next season, but anyway, shouldn't I be spending more time exercising or something . . . wait, where am I? I'm three miles past my exit, that's where!

Ten minutes of driving on autopilot. Yikes!

It's extremely frustrating and unsettling to know that I zone out like this sometimes. I want to be fully present at all times, but it's something I have to actively practice. Thankfully, my cognitive functions are only mildly impacted.

I have students who probably have this very sort of "missing time" experience, but for them, it happens consistently throughout the day. I can imagine what that must feel like for some students in our classrooms; they may want to be listening, following the lesson, but their minds just keep wandering. How frustrating it must be for them to feel lost every few minutes.

- Do you ever zone out while you're reading a novel and have to reread the last page or two? It may be challenging to ingest so much written language at once.

- Are you able to get work done on your laptop in a coffee shop or are the conversations around you too distracting? You may have difficulty filtering out background stimuli to focus on what's important.

- How much time can you spend on social media at one time? Five minutes? Ten? An hour? Maybe with certain media, you can intake more information at once than with other types.

- If you've skipped a meal, do you find it hard to focus on things? Maybe your body and mind can't afford to miss breakfast, and if you're hungry it affects your ability to concentrate at work.

Again, we're trying to find entry points into understanding our students' experiences in classrooms. If we can relate to their experiences, we can be more accurate in finding solutions. And remember, all of our students have a range of strengths and deficits in the areas

of input and production. And so, all of our students potentially benefit from engagement strategies.

How to Use This Book

Teach for Attention! has seven chapters, each of which focuses on
one major category of strategies for increasing engagement during
everyday classroom activities. The chapters describe a common
problem area experienced by students and teachers, explore why
students may have this challenge, and lay out the specific strategies
that target this issue. Think of these strategies as tools on your tool
belt. Some of them may be familiar to you, and you may even be
using them already, but you might find ideas or approaches that are
new to you. To that end, "Attention Grabbers"—real-world anecdotes
of memorable students I have worked with—support most of the
strategies. These short vignettes paint a picture of how these tools
actually work. The stories primarily cover reading, writing, and math,
spanning kindergarten through middle school. They are the heart of
this book, helping you recognize familiar scenarios and be able to
apply the ideas in your own classroom. While the students and their
stories are real, I have changed their names, and in a few cases, I have
combined similar students to make the concepts more clear.

While some of the stories come from my experience working
in classrooms as a support teacher or resource specialist, many of
them take place in one-to-one educational therapy sessions. While
this allows me certain luxuries a classroom teacher just doesn't
have—time, quiet, controlled environments—the tools do not
require that you spend lots of time sitting with various individual
students every day (which you probably do anyway if a student
needs significant help). They are supports you can inject into the
flow of your classroom, targeting as many students as you want. With

each anecdote—even if it happens in a controlled setting—I offer suggestions for how to implement the associated strategy in your classroom.

Each chapter also features one "Guest Speaker," an essay written by a general or special educator, an enrichment teacher, or an impacted student. These individuals share their own real-world stories of how different approaches resulted in better engagement. These help give different voices and perspectives on what attention support can look like in the classroom.

Finally, each chapter ends with "The Big Takeaway," summing up the salient points of the chapter.

You can read this book straight through, or you can use it as a reference or handbook by checking out different chapters based on what you think might work for you in your situation at a given time. Try lots of the ideas, and if one or two don't work well for you right away, try others. Having worked for years in schools of all kinds, I understand the absurd number of responsibilities and tasks teachers face on a daily basis. The ideas here can be done simply and with little preparation, which makes it easy to try them out. The strategies in this book do not require you to revamp your entire curriculum or change your whole style of teaching. Just pick tools that work for you, and use them.

An important key is playing offense, not defense, most of the time. That is, rather than using strategies after students have already failed, being proactive and building the strategies into the lessons or projects and/or making them part of the regular classroom workflow. It's also crucial to recognize if there are specific times or subjects that are especially challenging for students to engage with. For example, for students who can't attend to writing tasks, page 107 describes the benefits of using slide-making programs over word processing programs. But don't just use PowerPoint as standby support in case someone struggles. Build it in as an option for the assignment from the start. And do it for any project at all times.

For students with less severe challenges, you may not necessarily have to play offense all the time. With these students, you may notice a bit of difficulty with a particular lesson or project. In that case, throw in one of the simpler strategies that may serve as a jump start.

You can use any of these strategies with any student who struggles to connect with classroom material or assignments. Some of the strategies are more intensive, some less so, but you can adjust all of them to fit the needs of a particular student.

Engaging with Success

My hope is that these strategies work for you and your students. But if they don't exactly suit your needs or click with you, take the spirit of these suggestions and come up with your own ideas. Use your creativity. After all, every day you're up at the front of the room performing the lessons you've created. Teaching is a creative profession by nature!

> If we can put students in a position to experience some success in school and increase their self-confidence, it may be the most important component of their sustained engagement.

Perhaps even more important than creativity is empathy. Back in that teachers' meeting, I wanted to be attentive. I knew the material was important, but my brain just couldn't keep up. You don't have to sit in a lot of staff meetings to understand how hard it can be for students to stay engaged at school. You've lived it—we all have. When it comes to engagement, the kids are not the problem. The problem is that they're expected to sit inside classrooms every day for hours on end and perform on command. For many of them, this is like putting a hummingbird in a cage.

These students have so much to offer, but they've likely experienced a lot of failure in the classroom. If we can put them in a position to experience some success in school and increase their self-confidence, it may be the most important component of their sustained engagement. And from there, the opportunities for their achievement continue to grow.

I would love to hear how these strategies have worked for you, especially if you have modified them or come up with your own versions. If you would like to share your own Attention Grabbers, or if you have questions, please email me through Free Spirit Publishing at help4kids@freespirit.com.

Time to get engaged!

Ezra Werb

CHAPTER 1

GET INTEREST RATES UP
How to Incorporate Students' Personal Interests

We plan great lessons. Let's not be humble.

They're well structured. They're interactive. They're sequenced clearly. The content is interesting. There's plenty of repetition and practice built in. Most of our students seem alert, engaged, and able to complete the related independent work.

But sometimes certain students just can't sustain engagement with our teaching. They miss key ideas. They're confused. When it's time for them to put what they've learned into practice, they show you that blank look, as if they've been somewhere else. It's like there's no one operating their input controls. It may be happening throughout the day, or perhaps at specific times or during certain subjects.

We can more easily reach these kids if we use their own interests in our lessons. Consider how we work with struggling readers. Of course, teaching phonics and practicing fluency is imperative for students with dyslexia, but to motivate these students to engage in an activity that causes them to struggle, teachers and parents give them books that include their personal interests or high-interest material—in other words, books that kids would choose for themselves. This may be a graphic novel of a popular animated series or a video game handbook, a movie-spinoff chapter book or a YA novel about zombies. It works because the familiarity with the material eases stress and increases motivation.

We can apply this same reasoning to the classroom in general. Psychologist Dr. Robert Brooks coined the phrase "islands of competence" for those areas where people with disabilities shine, where they show skill, where they possess knowledge. Let's bring these islands into our classrooms. Students perk up when they already know something about what you're teaching. It's as if their personal interest makes them feel confident and helps fuel their mental energy, allowing their input abilities to work better.

To make use of students' interests, first we must find out what their interests are.

Get to Know Students' Interests

All of your students have interests. These are topics they know a lot about or activities in which they excel. If given the choice, they would spend most of their time just talking about these things. And because of that, it's usually not difficult to find out what your students are into. Here are some ways you can do that.

- **Surveys.** On day one or day 100 (it's never too late!), have students fill out a paper or an electronic survey. With kindergartners, you can ask them verbally or have their parents fill out a survey. Ask about their favorites: movies, TV shows, books, graphic novels, hobbies, activities, and so on. Students will be impressed that a teacher wants to know how much they love playing Mario Kart Racing, how they know all of Taylor Swift's lyrics, or how they're obsessed with a smartphone's hidden features.

- **Chat with students at recess.** Spend a few minutes with kids at recess. Students and teachers tend to loosen up as soon as the bell rings and everyone goes outside. It's a whole different vibe out there. Even just chatting with kids for a few minutes can tell you so much about them. You can ask what TV shows they're watching these days, what video game they're currently playing, or what after-school activities they're doing. You can also talk with them at other less-formal times, like during hall passing, on the bus for a field trip, or while waiting for pick up after school.

- **Listen in.** If you just hang around while students eat their snacks or chat at the beginning of class, you'll inevitably hear what they're passionate about at the moment. This seems like common sense, but downtime discourse often revolves around their interests. Do a little eavesdropping and you'll know what new game app your students just can't live without.

With surveys, all that information is recorded. If you're gleaning information through informal chats, take notes so you won't forget. This is valuable data!

For various reasons, some students may not be very forthcoming about their personal interests, and it can be harder to learn about them. Some kids are just shy. Other kids lack confidence or don't think their interests are worth sharing. If they've been struggling in school and feeling beat-up by the experience, they may feel it's too risky to share. But you can still discern their interests. If you're getting lots of "I don't knows" out of students you're trying to help, look for clues. They may have logos or images of characters on their clothing, lunchboxes, binders, or lockers. Maybe a student has an emoji keychain on his backpack. Try mentioning emojis in a lesson and see if his attention perks up. You can also talk to parents and guardians. No need to make a big deal out of it, but a quick email home asking what the student is into might turn up something helpful.

> Let students be the experts and use the confidence that comes from expertise to increase their attention and understanding.

So what do you do with this CIA briefing on your students? That's the fun part: You let them teach you. Allow students to be the experts and use the confidence that comes from expertise to increase attention and understanding.

This doesn't mean building entire lessons around their personal interests, just adding some bits—like throwing some chocolate chips into your morning cereal. Not too many, but enough to give it a kick. Throwing some chocolate chips into your lessons is easy and fun and tastes good.

There are two main ways to incorporate these bits into the curriculum, and they correspond to our *input* and *production* functions. You can use student interests to help them absorb new information (input) and effectively output content (production).

Input: Incorporate Their Interests Into Lessons

Just to emphasize, you're not going to have students read Captain Underpants as an introduction to literary analysis. But there are countless ways you can use him and characters like him in supporting roles in your lessons. You can always change the details of your discussions to add a bit of content your students care about, or use extra examples based on their entertainment loves. Here is an example.

ATTENTION GRABBER
Maleficent Math Problems

For students with input challenges, math word problems can induce nightmares—falling-off-a-building, stuck-in-a-maze caliber night-mares about quantities of things, and having to do something with those things, and just how many things do we have now?! It is very difficult for these students to input the language, input the numbers, and then process those two elements in conjunction to deduce what operation to use. And because it is so difficult for them, students often tune out immediately, their minds' way of giving up.

I once had a third-grade student, Veronica, in my resource group who was a huge fan of the Disney Channel movies, the *Descendants*; she had the books and accessories and all that. But she was having a real tough time making sense of word problems, and so she would stop listening whenever they came up. She wouldn't even attempt problems that had more than a few words in them.

Knowing she was such a fan of the magic-themed show, I rewrote a few of the problems incorporating some of the characters into them. Here's one of the original problems: "If Becky already has 12 flowers and her mother gives her ⅓ as many, will she have enough total flowers to put into 18 vases?"

And here's how I rewrote it, incorporating characters from the Disney show: "Mal and Evie are preparing for a slumber party. Mal uses magic to create 12 cupcakes. Evie uses her magic to create ⅓ as many. Together, will they have enough if 18 guests are coming over?"

Immediately, Veronica smiled and started telling me about the show. We started talking about the characters and how they use magic, and I allowed her a minute to tell me all about it. She was very expressive when it came to something she knew a lot about. Then, when I prompted her to read the problem, she was quicker and more energetic to do so. After reading it, she needed some reteaching for how to draw pictures to help her figure out the problem, but she got it. Once she was connected to the material, it was easier to reteach her the steps to solve it.

I realize that this is a small, simple adjustment. Perhaps it seems almost trite. But I've rarely seen teachers do it, and it's too easy *not* to try. Don't underestimate how effective even a slight change can make in reaching students. Throw in a problem with some characters they like, and they feel comfortable because with these characters, they're experts. Invite Peppa Pig and the PAW Patrol into your math lessons and watch your kindergartners' eyes light up.

Wikipedia. You may not want to use it for scholarly research, but it comes in handy for quick learning about your students' interests.

By the way, how did I know about Mal and Evie? Wikipedia. You may not want to use it for scholarly research, but it comes in handy for quick learning about your students' interests. Once I got the idea, I looked up the *Descendants* during a spare moment and scanned the characters section. It took about two minutes of grueling research.

Using students' interests can be an especially effective tool in English language arts. For example, when we teach story elements like character, conflict, plot, and setting, we pick a story the students are familiar with to dissect the pieces and highlight their meaning.

Sure, you could use your read-aloud book or maybe something they read last year. But for struggling readers, these references might not be as engaging as a movie they just saw over the weekend.

If you ask for volunteers to recap a new kid-trendy movie, students who never volunteer for anything involving language arts may suddenly want to tell you every plot detail of the movie. Now that they're engaged and confident, you can generalize the narrative elements to any story, and soon enough, to whatever book you're reading in class.

The technique of using movies works for older students as well. When teaching literature in middle school classrooms, explaining the concept of a story's theme can be tricky. It's not a moral or a message, necessarily; it's the idea and concept the story is centered around. Students with attention difficulties expend a lot of mental energy just to input all of the story information while reading, which makes the more abstract, higher-order thinking that much more challenging. Often, this is where they lose engagement with the material.

But it can be really effective to reference movies to engage students in the process of text analysis. For those into superheroes and comic books, discuss how the X-Men movies center around themes of conformity versus individuality as well as society's acceptance of people's differences. You could show your students how *Wonder Woman* is a meditation on war or how *Toy Story* is about identity and agency. I once had a student who loved *Rocky*, so we figured out that it's a movie about a working-class hero and the ambition to rise above one's social status.

Sports are another common student passion. Wherever you teach, you will almost certainly have sports fans among your students. Whether you're a fan or not, it's easy to catch up on big sports events or athletes and use that information to help kids digest lessons.

ATTENTION GRABBER

Proper and Common Nouns Are a Slam Dunk

Anthony, a second grader with a terrific sense of humor, also had severe attention issues among other undiagnosed processing difficulties. As a result, he was barely hanging on in an academically rigorous private school. As a resource specialist, I spent time in his classroom supporting a few of the students with learning challenges, including Anthony, while the teacher taught lessons. During direct instruction, he struggled greatly with input; he could only attend to the classroom teacher for about a minute at a time, even when the lessons were simple.

He also happened to be a sports fan, and I knew what did hold his attention: a certain NBA team. He often wore a Golden State Warriors hat to school, which he begrudgingly took off every morning before he came into class.

Up front, the teacher was explaining the difference between common and proper nouns. She had some standard examples on the T-chart: girl, Sarah; state, California; planet, Jupiter. Straightforward stuff, but Anthony was clearly not absorbing any of it. I stepped up behind him, kneeled close, and whispered: "What about Stephen Curry?"

He instantly perked up. "You know who he is?" he asked.

"Of course I do. He's one of the best players in the NBA. And Stephen Curry is a proper noun. The common noun is *basketball player*."

"Ohhhhh," he said, the light bulb going *ping* over his head.

Now I had his attention. "What about the name of his team?" I asked.

"The Warriors," he said.

"Right. *Warriors* is the proper noun. Proper nouns are names. The common noun is *team*. It says what the proper noun is naming."

This exchange seemed to jump-start his mind. Not only was he attentive and participating for the remainder of the lesson, he was able to independently complete the worksheet afterward, outputting information using the new skill he'd learned.

It worked because Anthony could be confident in his knowledge. And, of course, talking about his favorite sports team made him feel like he was relaxing at home on his couch watching a Warriors game. Feeling confident and relaxed can increase a student's engagement to the point where it lasts through independent work time as well.

The whole intervention with Anthony took thirty seconds, and I thought of it on the spot—no prep necessary. You can drop references to specific students' interests easily in one-to-one moments with students like Anthony, but you can use this tool just as easily in your lessons for the whole class; the proper names T-chart could have included "basketball team, Warriors."

Of course, students' interests go well beyond sports and entertainment, and you can tap into all sorts of student passions to help them digest lessons. Students have wide-ranging and often surprising hobbies, from gardening to baking, commercial airliners to online video gaming, horse care to skateboarding. I've known a male student who was into sewing and a female third grader who was into horror movies. It seems that *Magic: The Gathering* is still hanging around. Many kids enjoy athletic activities like martial arts, dance, and parkour.

Whatever hobbies students have, you can engage them by referencing these islands of competence during lessons. Even video games can be a legitimate way to engage students.

ATTENTION GRABBER

Stock Market for Gamers

I was working after school with an eighth grader with ADHD who had written a short research paper about the 1929 stock market crash. Alexander did a bare-bones job of culling some information from the internet and weaving it into a summary. It was clear from his demeanor and tone he had zero interest in the stock market. What the heck did he care if it crashed 100 years ago, or whatever, and can't we just talk about the new *God of War* game? He was a huge online gamer and was extremely knowledgeable on the subject.

I asked him if he understood what the stock market is and what the crash really meant, and he quickly said he had no idea. As I began explaining how stocks are traded on the market, he made a connection to something he cared about. He told me about an online video game where players can buy and sell digital items to use within the game. He explained that it wasn't the game company that facilitated the trading but a third-party site where people would post their items for sale and buyers would come looking, like Craigslist. He went even further and spoke about how the prices of the items would fluctuate depending on the demand for them.

During this conversation, I could almost see the neurons firing in his brain. He was engaged because he had made a connection to something with which he was an expert, something that greatly interested him, and in the process, he had grasped a pretty complex concept. We proceeded to have an in-depth discussion about the market crash and consequences of it: What if everyone pulled their money out of the online gaming exchange? Would the digital items have any value?

In this case, I didn't plan anything; the student brought his own interest to the table without being prompted. If we show interest in students' hobbies and passions, talk to them about video games, movies, or whatever they're into, we open the door for them to make connections like this and share them in class.

Production: Let Students Be Experts in the Work They Produce

Students can be intense about their interests. Not only do they love certain aspects of culture—music, movies, fashion, sports, and so on—but they can often tell you every little detail about them. They've done their research, they've thought deeply, and their strong opinions are proof of this.

Inspiring kids to care this strongly about anything academic? Not as easy. But if we let them produce content related to their interests, we get buy in.

ATTENTION GRABBER
Adding *Gravity* to Venn Diagrams

Sasha was a fourth grader diagnosed with ADHD and high-functioning autism, and I was providing in-class academic support for her and some other students. She loved talking about animated TV series and could tell you all about the characters, their histories, and what they liked for breakfast. She wasn't so interested in academic topics.

The teacher was reading *The Phantom Tollbooth* with the students, and she was introducing Venn diagrams. This being a tool for comprehension, it was one Sasha would truly benefit from. Graphic organizers like Venn diagrams, cause-effect charts, and story maps present information clearly so students can input the information and make sense of it (these are discussed further in chapter 6). But for

Sasha, a Venn diagram was just some abstract art that wasn't relevant to her. Furthermore, she had been struggling to engage with the novel—the language was difficult, and she was getting tripped up with the wordplay.

My main objective was to get her attention focused on *Tollbooth* and the new concept map. So I helped introduce the Venn diagram to the class by asking Sasha to compare Milo, the main character of the novel, to Dipper Pines, the main character of her favorite animated show, *Gravity Falls.*

I blinked, and she was at the whiteboard, marker in hand, adding information to all three sections of the chart. Because she was interested in the content, her input abilities were fully functioning, allowing her to learn a new concept. As a result, she was able to output knowledge she already possessed, fusing it with the new skill she'd just learned.

Here's the value added to using this sort of strategy. In her mind, Sasha may always be wondering if and when I will be referencing her favorite show again, or maybe another show she loves. In the ensuing weeks, we did drop in *Gravity Falls* references intermittently, when it made sense to do so.

And her anticipation grew, along with her sustained attention to lessons.

Of course, it's not always a smooth process when we bring student interests into the classroom. In fact, when I first tried to engage Sasha by mentioning her favorite TV show in class, prior to the Venn diagram lesson, it was a disaster. I had planned to announce during the lesson that *The Phantom Tollbooth* had some things in common with *Gravity Falls*. I figured just mentioning the show would get her interested and lead to her participation in the discussion. So I proposed that the strange, mysterious quality of the universe of *The Phantom Tollbooth* was similar to that of *Gravity Falls*, another world where bizarre things happened.

Sasha perked up at the mention of her favorite show, but the problem was what happened next. She proceeded to explain how the show was really nothing like this book.

Well, okay, at least she was interested and comparing the two stories. But then she went off on tangents about the show, and they had nothing to do with our discussion or the novel. And she just kept going. It was tricky, because the lead teacher and I were pleased that she was engaged, but her attention was now focused primarily on the show itself, outside the scope of our lesson. And of course, this distracts other students, and before you know it, it's *Gravity Falls* 101.

This isn't entirely a loss. Sasha was attentive to something classroom related, which was a victory. But I clearly needed to re-strategize. I realized it was key to bring in high interests in a more formal, structured manner. That's why the Venn diagram lesson worked. Sasha could still be thinking about her favorite show and display her knowledge but do so within the structure of our lesson.

We're all bound to run into some initial failures when trying new strategies. But those failures can be teaching moments, and with course correction, we can make adjustments and find the way.

Teenagers often have even more passion for their interests than younger kids. And it's usually not hard to get them excited about producing work that focuses on those passions.

Consider the persuasive essay. The goal is to get students to think deeply about a topic, arrive at a strong point of view, dissect the topic from multiple angles, find evidence, explain that evidence with coherent writing, and ultimately, make a compelling, articulate argument defending their ideas.

Simple, right? Okay, maybe not—especially for kids who do the bulk of their communication in thumb-typed, fractured phrases with misspelled words and acronyms for lewd language. Factor in attention-related issues like mental energy or production difficulties, and the task of getting certain students excited about writing a persuasive essay can be formidable.

So, before you ask students to produce an essay about something more abstract and complicated—like whether nature or nurture determines a person's life course or whether cloning is morally sound or whether capital punishment is a just system—start by asking them about something they already understand and feel strongly about.

ATTENTION GRABBER
Skating into Persuasion
Kai was a middle school student who I was working with after school. He was able to write clear sentences but putting his attention toward a complete five-paragraph essay was not happening. He was just not interested. I knew he was a huge skateboarding and X-Games fanatic, so I posed this question to him: Who is the greatest big ramp rider of all time, Tony Hawk or Bob Burnquist?

Of course, he was all over this.

He quickly brainstormed various reasons why Hawk was totally the greatest, and anyone who didn't think so was obviously a poseur. Using an essay outline frame, I guided him to begin constructing paragraphs. His interest was high as he searched for facts online to ensure he was including correct information. As he worked, he kept telling me more facts about the two skateboarders, working out the argument in his head.

After completing the essay, Kai turned to me and said the following: "I wish I could write about skateboarding for class assignments."

Yes, because I was seeing him in a one-to-one setting outside the classroom, I had the luxury of time. And obviously you have course material you have to get through. Skateboarding is surely not in the lesson plan. Again, I'm not advocating changing the content of your curriculum. But if your goal is teaching students how to construct a persuasive essay, why not remove obstacles—such as complicated content material—that have nothing to do with those skills? Before you get to the more complex writing tasks, first hook them into the writing process by allowing them to express themselves about a topic that's related to their personal interests. Maybe they could extol the qualities of Instagram versus Snapchat as a means of communication. Or argue why they feel video games should or should not have a rating system.

Another approach to this is to model the writing process for the class as a whole-group exercise using a high-interest topic. Or perhaps break your class into two groups and have each compose an essay taking opposing sides of an argument. One side argues that iPhones are the best handheld devices. The other side argues for Androids. You can bet this is going to be a heated argument.

Then, when they have to write about a more complex topic that requires some background information, ethical thinking, and analysis, at the very least they will already be engaged with the writing process and feel comfortable with it. At best, they might find out they're pretty good at writing persuasive essays or even that they enjoy it.

The following guest speaker used a high-interest topic to help a student's math production, taking this concept even further.

GUEST SPEAKER
LAURA BAHR

Laura Bahr teaches at a school for twice-exceptional students; each student is gifted cognitively but also has learning or developmental challenges. She currently works with high schoolers on special projects, but she taught middle school math for years. Here, she talks about how she used Minecraft *to grab the attention of one of her anxious math students.*

For my middle school students, single-step problems were usually a piece of cake, but multistep algebraic equations made some of them anxious. One particular student had a great deal of math-related anxiety and attention issues. He would say he was "terrible at math" and write insults like "I am so stupid" on worksheets when he struggled.

One assignment was to demonstrate understanding of how to solve multistep equations. I knew this student wouldn't be able to show that on paper or the whiteboard, and honestly, I couldn't even tell at that point if he could do any sort of algebra problems because he could barely stand to look at them.

One thing he *did* attend to was the video game *Minecraft*, which he loved almost obsessively. If you're not familiar, *Minecraft* is a sandbox game, meaning players can interact with the content any way they want to—there are no rules, and play is based on open-ended choice. *Minecraft* is also a building game, so players build their world and interact with it how they like.

So I asked my student to do a project in *Minecraft*. His assignment was the same as before, to explain each part of solving two-step equations, but he could build the lesson in a virtual world he created.

He was immediately excited by the idea, asking me questions about what he could and couldn't do for the assignment. Because his anxiety was lowered and he was actually listening to me, we were able to go through each of the steps of several difficult example equations. We were looking for the perfect one for him to teach.

Once he had identified the equation he wanted to use, he used his expertise with the game app to construct a block classroom in the virtual environment. He designed a guided tour and then brought the viewer to a chalkboard where the different equations were provided. I still didn't know at this point if he actually could solve them, but soon enough, in the virtual classroom he built, he also showed the process for solving the equations.

Now that he was managing the algebra, I asked him also to make up some examples from scratch and encouraged him to play with the levels of difficulty to provide as examples for other students: Do we want our variable to be a whole number? Do we want to use negative coefficients for this example?

This project made him realize that he actually had a knack for solving equations and he enjoyed the puzzle aspect of finding solutions. Solving equations became the area in which he had the most confidence and success in math on future quizzes and tests.

I honestly don't know how else I would have found this out. His anxiety and attention issues were so severe with solving equations that I had to find some way in. *Minecraft* turned out to be the thing he needed.

Laura's story takes me by surprise. I would expect math teachers to use *Minecraft,* which is focused on building, to explore geometry and measurement standards; algebra and *Minecraft* aren't clearly connected. But using his expertise in the game as a way to present his output lowered this student's anxiety and increased his motivation. It is worth considering other methods of presentation that might work with students' interests. Your kids who love YouTube videos might be interested in recording their English "essay" in video format. Perhaps a drama student can give a soliloquy dressed as a character from history. A visual artist might be able to paint a poster describing a geometric proof. The possibilities are as broad as your student population.

Keeping It Appropriate

Sometimes you will run into students whose main interests are in topics that aren't appropriate for the classroom. This might be a mature TV series that some of your kids are streaming, a violent video game, or something else. This may present a problem, especially if you've set a precedent of giving class attention to the interests of other students. You don't want to minimize or denigrate the interests of any of your students, but you also can't devote class time to something that is violent or otherwise inappropriate.

It's a tightrope, but you can usually just level with students if it comes up: For example, "We have a strict policy against talking about guns and violence as entertainment in class." Of course, if this is with older students, and you're discussing this topic in a mature manner, that's another story. You will need to be the judge of what's appropriate, keeping your student population, your principal, your school district, and your own personal comfort level in mind.

As far as violent video games are concerned, there are usually other aspects to these games than just violence—things that might be appropriate and helpful to a student. Often teamwork is involved. Strategy. Some games take place in a real historical context and can lead kids to wanting to learn more. Some games take place in interesting environments or have intriguing stories. One of my students loves a particularly violent game, but he did a project for class where he analyzed how the game uses percentages and other math domains. It might be worth talking to your student during recess or another break to learn what aspects of the game might be appropriate and applicable to your class content. The student is likely to understand your perspective, especially if you show willingness to talk about some elements of the game. If it doesn't work out, and the student is too fixated on the game's violent aspects, you'll have to firmly uphold your policy. See if you can find another entry point to the student's interests.

The Big Takeaway

All of us have interests and activities in which we excel: movies, sports, comics, animals, trivia, sewing, jump rope, online gaming, cooking, crafts, and so on. And don't our interests engage us?

When teachers call attention to their students' personal interests, it tells the students that they, too, have ideas worth sharing—and it tells them that the teacher cares enough to include them in the classroom. This can perpetuate further participation because now their distracted brains have motivation to *attend*—not just to enjoy speaking and hearing about their high-interest subject weaved into lessons, but also to experience more moments of feeling like an expert in the immediate future.

Using students' interests can be an effective tool for both their inputting of information and their producing of work. Find ways for students to connect to your material.

Use *Finding Dory* to teach about plot structure.

Use Legos to teach about geometry.

Have your elementary students fill out a character traits chart using their favorite *Avengers* superheroes or *Monster High* characters.

Have middle school students write a persuasive essay about whether junk food should be banned from school.

It's a simple strategy that can have a big payoff. And using students' interests is applicable to many other strategies in this book. The only real prep work involves getting to know what the kids are into . . .

. . . and maybe a bit of reconnaissance on Wikipedia.

CHAPTER 2

PLAY THE CONFIDENCE GAME
How to Raise Self-Esteem and Reduce Stress

When I was in tenth grade, I joined my temple's youth league basketball team. Though I was a solid player on the playground, I found myself completely stifled during league games. I was nervous and shaky. I dropped passes. I had the ball stolen from me. I missed easy shots. When I stepped onto that court, I had no confidence. And I wasn't having fun.

But one night during practice, something changed. We had just found out we hadn't qualified for the playoffs, so the pressure was very low. During our scrimmage, I found myself playing more aggressively than usual, driving to the hoop and hitting a few jump shots. One of the senior players pulled me aside.

"Where have you been all season?" he asked. "All of a sudden you decide to show us what you got? Kid, you gotta play like that during actual games."

Those words were like a confidence jolt. At that moment, I realized that I had been playing with fear. The following year, I remember psyching myself up for the first game, thinking back to what that senior had said. I stepped onto the court like I owned the place. (Such as it was—I mean, it was a tiny, decrepit gym with a busted scoreboard and roughly four people in the crowd . . . not exactly Madison Square Garden.) The first couple minutes, I played like I had in practice that night, and it just rolled from there. For the rest of the season, I played with confidence and had my best season by far. Not only did I play much better, but I had a lot of fun with my teammates. What a different experience from the previous year.

Reflecting on that memory, it's clear to me how things like pressure, verbal praise, fear, and confidence all factor into our successes and failures, especially when we're young and just starting to figure ourselves out.

Students with attention difficulties experience a lot of failure in school. With every unfinished assignment and failed quiz or test, they are further confronted with their own inadequacies. Many of the students with ADHD who I've known vocalize their lack of confidence, saying things like "I'm just stupid" or "I can't do it."

Other students seem to present an overconfidence even at times of great challenge, as they attempt to speed through assignments and be the first to declare, "Finished!" Researchers have even found that some students with ADHD experience a "positive illusory bias." That is, when asked about their own abilities and successes, they tend to rate them higher than their performance in those areas would suggest. Many theories have been studied about what might cause this, with no conclusive results. One possibility is that these students are compensating for the weaknesses they perceive in themselves by attempting to mask these weaknesses in confidence.

Either way, whether students lack confidence or are overconfident for unsubstantiated reasons, confidence is something we should focus on.

How does students' self-confidence play into their achievement?

According to a three-year longitudinal study started in 2003 with first-grade students, academic achievement may be more depen-dent on positive self-perceptions than on the willingness to learn. In other words, perceived competence is related to achievement in reading and math.[3] The researchers also summarize the findings of other studies, saying that achieving successes helps maintain con-fident students' self-perceptions, while failures will do the oppo-site for less-confident students. Furthermore, students may con-sequently take more effort or be more passive depending on their own self-evaluation of whether they can handle a task.

These studies were done with students without cognitive or developmental deficits. But it makes logical sense that any of us would be more apt to want to engage with new material if we are confident; our input controls are primed to take in new information. Those who lack confidence are

probably less likely to put forth any mental effort, given their history of failure. It's as if their anxiety is telling them not to participate.

These ideas are at the core of what educational therapists do. We support struggling students by helping alleviate fear and anxiety related to schoolwork and boosting their self-esteem by setting them up for incremental successes.

If we can create moments and opportunities for students to experience success and increase their confidence, even in small doses, they may be more likely to take an active role in their own learning and put more mental energy toward tasks.

So what can we do to make these moments of confidence happen?

Create Incremental Successes

Obviously, we want every student to reach certain standards, and each one should have the opportunity to do so. We want to raise the bar so our students can improve. Often, though, the way to start struggling students on this path is by setting realistic goals they can meet. That doesn't mean lowered expectations. We're trying to build confidence, and the way to do that is by creating opportunities for students to succeed.

ATTENTION GRABBER
Spelling Test Success

I was providing academic support in a third-grade classroom. Celeste, one of my students, was an extremely creative and social girl who also had severe dyslexia and attention challenges that made reading and spelling very difficult. Our first spelling test was relatively easy; we were just trying to get a baseline on students' abilities, but Celeste couldn't keep up. I had to constantly repeat the words for her, with her attention wavering for the duration of the test. And she didn't get any of the words correct.

Celeste didn't seem upset—it was more like she'd expected to fail, so for her this was just routine. She knew how poorly she did without even seeing the corrected test.

And I didn't show it to her. There would be no benefit to her seeing the abundant amount of circled misspellings—it was simply too much for her to learn at that point—and it would most likely be another hit to her self-esteem. Instead, I came up with a plan to get her up and running on the spelling tests.

The following week, I only gave her five out of the ten spelling words to study and explained that she would only need to remember these for the test. She smiled, appearing immediately relieved. That week, I made her flash cards with the five words on them, with the phonics patterns highlighted so they were easier to recognize.

On Friday during the spelling test, Celeste only had to exert mental energy for the five words I'd assigned to her, and she was able to remain engaged with the test. Having only five words to focus on also allowed her to feel capable enough to really give those words her best shot. She spelled three out of five correctly, a big improvement from zero out of ten. I showed the test to her, and she was very impressed with herself, showing it to classmates with pride.

Some argue that the way to get struggling students up to the level of their classmates is to maintain the same rigor, so they reach upward. This wasn't going to happen with Celeste. If I had continued to give her all ten words, I'm pretty sure she would have continued to get zeroes. The combination of dyslexia, attention issues, and low confidence would have deterred her from even trying, especially after the failure on that first test.

Students with these sorts of challenges need to feel successful in the academic tasks they struggle with. With fewer words to learn,

Celeste experienced some success, and as the weeks went on, she started to get four and then five out of five correct on the tests. Then I increased the difficulty by adding another two words for her to study, raising the total to seven words for the tests.

And then I added another . . . and another . . .

Until she was attempting all ten words.

By the end of the year, she may not have been scoring ten out of ten—more like six or seven on average—and she still needed words repeated for her. But she was taking the full tests like her peers.

More importantly, she was trying her best to learn new words because she was confident enough to feel like she could do it.

Related to the topic of incremental goals and anxiety reduction, it can be incredibly helpful for some students to have a quiz or an exam broken up into pieces. If you think a given test might overwhelm a student due to its length and complexity, have the student only do a portion at a given time. Yes, this will prolong the process for the student overall, but tackling the test in increments could make it feel much more manageable and thus may produce better results. This might require some students to have to stay in at recess or lunch for the extra time, and they may be bummed about that, but it is to their benefit to have the extra sessions. And you can let them snack away while they work.

You can also apply the principal of creating incremental successes to any classwork or homework. Pages 91–95 lay out specific suggestions for creating realistic, incremental writing goals for the expected length of paragraphs or essays. For math, it would entail reducing the number of homework problems and then slowly increasing the volume as the student gains confidence. In any science class, it may mean reducing the amount of new vocabulary a student needs to memorize for a weekly quiz, and again, slowly increasing the amount as the student progresses.

It is also important to make sure students recognize their progress. When they do improve their production and accuracy, whether on classwork, quizzes, or essays, show them comparisons of their past and present work so they can see how they're improving.

Highlight Students' Strengths

To help students feel successful, you can also create opportunities for them to use and show off their strengths and abilities. Consider what your students *can* do.

Maybe a student has a drawing talent. The next time you need something drawn on the board, call on this student to help you in your lesson while also showing off the talent in front of classmates.

> Create opportunities for students to use and show off their strengths and abilities. Consider what your students *can* do.

Perhaps a student is good at chess. Might there be a way to relate this to geometry or multiplication? Could the student help you explain how historical conflicts could be seen through the lens of chess strategy?

If a student is funny and enjoys public speaking, perhaps that student can help you teach a lesson—and even help liven it up with some humor.

This strategy can be very effective in setting up students for success with more extensive class projects.

GUEST SPEAKER
MARY MCINERNEY

Mary McInerney has worked in the field of special education for many years. While continuing to teach students with learning exceptionalities, she also implements teacher development focusing on strength-based approaches. Here she tells a story about giving her elementary students options for presenting a science project.

In my fourth- and fifth-grade self-contained class, we had learned about the circulatory system. As an end-of-unit assessment, I wanted students to define key terms and vocabulary, label the system's components, and understand its overall function. Given my students' learning and attention struggles, I couldn't just have them all write research papers or take a multiple choice test, because most would have failed. It would have appeared they'd learned nothing, and I knew this wasn't true.

Considering their variety of skills and strengths—some were great artists or actors while others were better with design and construction—I offered them a menu of options for this project to demonstrate what they'd learned. This gave them choices for presentation that suited their strengths, areas in which they felt confident.

Victor was a child who had been in other schools where they just thought he couldn't learn or produce anything. His self-esteem was very low. When challenged by any assignment, certainly any writing task, he would just shut down. Often, he would avoid challenges by falling asleep in class or hiding away in the beanbag area. He would totally opt out, no negotiation. However, we'd noticed throughout the year that he learned better while watching videos on the computer.

Throughout this unit, my co-teacher and I prompted Victor to gather information online with an app that had three-dimensional models of organs. He was especially fascinated with related diseases in which the circulatory system breaks down. Knowing his own visual-spatial strengths, he chose to create a model for his project, similar to ones he saw in videos on the website. That was the key decision for him: picking the manner of presentation he felt confident with. Next, he figured out the exact topic—angioplasty—and started planning. I gave him a checklist of what knowledge he needed to demonstrate.

He went straight to work, first making a list of needed materials. This included a big cardboard tube for the artery, a balloon for the stent, a thinner clear tube to blow up the balloon, and an obstruction to blow out of the artery. Once he constructed it all, he presented it to the class using the appropriate terms and procedures to demonstrate his learned knowledge. His peers were amazed, giving him positive feedback, and this made him feel very proud.

A few of my students chose to act out doing an actual surgery, dressed in scrubs and using a skeletal model. One student created a comic strip about a doctor performing surgery. Another made little sculptures of organs out of modeling clay.

All of these students demonstrated that they knew the material. They just needed a way to output it with confidence. Working within their skill sets, they were intrinsically motivated, and I was able to accurately assess what they'd learned.

Mary's story perfectly represents what strength-based education really means, and it can be so effective in raising students' confidence. We also see here that she used Victor's strengths not just in producing work with his model, but as an entry point to the material by having him watch videos and see 3-D models online.

Some students learn better visually, while others better ingest material auditorily. Still others prefer to input information through kinesthetic or tactile activities; they need to have their bodies moving and/or be able to touch things to understand them. In Mary's story, Victor is a visual learner who needed to see the 3-D models online, and he's a student who produces better by building. But every student has a different strength profile. And when students are working with their strengths, whether inputting or producing material, they may feel more confident.

I've known students who were really into music, either as musicians or fans. Whenever possible, I played tunes related to what we were studying. Whether I was playing Schoolhouse Rock! songs to teach students about parts of speech, science-themed songs from the band They Might Be Giants, or Natalie Merchant's song "Wonder" for a student who was reading R.J. Palacio's novel *Wonder* (whose title was inspired by the song), the idea was for auditory learners (or music lovers) to feel confident as soon as they heard the first musical notes. Music is their preferred domain, and playing a song that either explains something or connects to the lesson connects them immediately to the material.

The key is to recognize that you have many different kinds of learners in your class, so the most effective move is to present material in different ways so that all learning styles are covered.

Use Reinforcement Systems Effectively

Positive Behavior Interventions and Supports (PBIS) has become the standard approach to both schoolwide and classroom management systems. The principles of PBIS are that we shouldn't merely react to behavior problems with punishments but create an environment where students actively learn the appropriate ways to behave in various social settings. Furthermore, if there are undesirable behaviors, the goal is to figure out the function of the behavior—what purpose it serves the child—and find alternative ways for the student to fulfill that want or need. Perhaps most important, teachers should find ways to positively reinforce appropriate behavior, either through tangible rewards or verbal praise.

The ability to control one's impulses and foresee consequences of one's actions are often weak in students with the hyperactive-impulsive type of ADHD. This often results in a lot of reprimands and punishments from teachers and parents. Imagine how damaging it can be to students' self-esteem to be punished for impulses they're not currently capable of controlling. But we can find ways to incorporate positive behavior supports into our classrooms. Within behavior reinforcement systems, we can make specific adjustments and tweaks to ensure that these students are benefiting from them.

In elementary school classrooms, teachers often use two different kinds of reinforcement systems: one for the whole class and one for individual students. They can employ both systems at the same time, and they can use multiple versions of each. It's worth examining each system to figure out how each one can benefit students with attention challenges specifically and how we can adjust to avoid pitfalls.

If any of your students have significant behavioral challenges, ones that suggest social/emotional issues or ones so pervasive that the student's academic and social functioning are severely impaired, it is imperative that you consult with parents and administrators and seek out appropriate professional support. The strategies here are meant for raising confidence and engagement in students showing mild-to-moderate behavior challenges typical of students with attention challenges or ADHD.

For those worried that reinforcement systems result in students showing appropriate behavior only to earn tangible rewards, it's important to remember that we should always have our eye on phasing out tangible reinforcements methodically over time. Ultimately, we want students to internalize the behaviors so they don't need outside help with them, but reinforcement and reward systems are effective ways to get there.

Whole-Class Systems

Marble jars and similar behavior reinforcement tools treat the whole class as a unit, reinforcing everyone's collective positive behavior by rewarding behaviors such as respecting a teacher with hand raising instead of calling out, cleaning up after a project, coming back quietly from recess, transitioning calmly to a specialist's class, and so on. When the jar is full—or when a certain number of stickers have been put on a chart, or whatever the system is—the teacher rewards the class with a prize, often a party or event of some sort.

For students who exhibit problems with impulsive behavior, you can use the class reinforcement tool as a way to boost their confidence in their own abilities to regulate themselves and behave in the expected manner. These students are often blamed for things even when they don't do anything wrong. For example, if the class loses a marble because students were being loud while lining up, a student with a history of making noise in line may get the blame even if it wasn't that student who did it. With the marble jar, try to reverse these sorts of negative impressions of a student by finding opportunities when this student does something really positive and adding a marble while announcing to the class, "I'm giving the whole class a marble because Eva swept the floor after our project, and no one even asked her to do it." Not only will this make Eva feel great about herself for earning the marble for everyone, her classmates are more likely to see her as someone who can contribute positively to the class.

The flip side of this happens when we take out marbles from the jar for one student's actions. This inherently puts that student in the spotlight, except this time it makes the student feel more like he has committed a crime. One might argue that this could help curb that behavior for that student, and others, in the future. But remember, our students may have significant impulse control problems. They may have to try three times as hard as their peers to foresee consequences and control impulses. Punishing them for this, along with the whole class, will likely only serve to lower their self-esteem and sustain the negative perception peers have of them.

I have been guilty of this. Sometimes our frustrations get to us in the moment and *we* act impulsively as well. When I have made this error and realized my misstep, I tried to find a time as soon as possible when the student could earn back a marble for the class.

Marble jars can increase the self-esteem of students by providing instant positive feedback for proper behaviors. But consider these guidelines.

Marble Jar Do's and Don'ts

1. DO use the marble jar primarily to reinforce the actions of the entirety or majority of your class. Ideally, you're also using it as a team-building strategy. However . . .

2. DO put marbles in the jar when a particular student with attention or impulsivity issues shows positive behavior, even if others don't at that time. And, by all means, make a show of it. It is worth making it an individual reward system in that moment because the potential self-esteem and social gains are significant.

3. DON'T use it to target individual students who struggle behavior-ally. If a student with impulse control challenges is the only one not showing on-task behavior, DO NOT take out marbles from the jar and make that student the "spoiler."

Individual Student Systems

Many teachers refer to reward systems that target the behavior of individual students as "class currency," so let's call it that. These can take the form of tickets or fake money. Obviously, the objects won't qualify as currency unless they grant the students purchasing power in the classroom economy. And so, we have the class store. Most teachers set up a store on Fridays, designating a few tables in the back or side of the room to lay out items students can purchase with their earned dollars or tickets; these often include supplies like pencils, sharpeners and erasers with fun designs; crayon sets; coloring books; little stuffed animals; and other inexpensive toys. Students can "go shopping" in groups of three or four and purchase items, reinforcing the value of the currency (it's also a good way to practice math skills).

The idea with class currency is to target specific behaviors that may happen throughout the day or that occur at specific times. It may be that a student doesn't put completed homework in the designated box. Maybe a student always calls out answers to math problems before classmates get the chance to try answering it. A student might be actively bothering a neighbor or interrupting your lessons by calling out off-topic statements.

For students with impulse control challenges, it is especially important to speak with them about those behaviors and discuss possible replacement behaviors—raising a hand instead of calling out, for example. And then reinforce their new actions or impulse control with class currency.

ATTENTION GRABBER
Ticket for a Quiet Signal

My third-grade student with attention challenges, Jasmine, was a very social kid who would talk to anybody. After recess and lunch, our class policy was to enter the room quietly, take out materials, and get ready for the next subject, but Jasmine struggled to control her impulse to continue her conversations from outside. I had already suggested the replacement behavior of having her finish the conversations in the snack area with whomever she was talking to, but either the friend would want to enter class immediately, prompting Jasmine to keep talking, or they would end up staying outside for ten minutes.

We had a class currency system in the form of tickets, so I told her I would be looking for her to control her need to talk after walking in the room and that I would reward her with tickets if she could do it. At the end of the next recess, I reminded her quickly about her new earning potential, and she came in quietly, sat down, and put her "quiet signal" up in the air: a peace sign with one hand and the forefinger of her other hand pressed to her mouth.

So far, so good.

The next recess, I did not remind her, and she was right back to talking as she entered the room, seemingly louder than ever before. Other students around her had their quiet signals up, attempting to ignore her talking, and so I went over to them and gave them each a ticket. Upon seeing this, she was reminded of the deal, and she immediately stopped talking and raised her quiet signal.

It went like this for a couple of days. Sometimes Jasmine would enter quietly and earn a ticket. Other times she would forget. Then, after about a week, she seemed to turn a corner. She was consistently walking in quietly and raising her quiet signal, even when others were talking around her.

She earned a lot of tickets over the next few weeks.

Eventually, I phased out giving her tickets by awarding them less frequently, but the new behavior stuck regardless if she earned a ticket or not. The next time the class store was open, she took her time deciding which item her sister would enjoy the most as a birthday present.

Here are confidence-building guidelines for class currency systems for individuals.

Class Currency Guidelines

1. DO award currency for very specific behaviors.

2. DO focus the reward system on one or two particular behaviors at a time for students with severe impulse control issues. It may be too difficult for them to control all of their impulses consistently throughout the day. Highlighting one or two behaviors helps these students focus their mental energy on specific tasks.

3. DO use a prize box or class store regularly. The more the students have fun with whatever tchotchkes they buy at your little class market, the more motivating the tickets will become.

4. DO put in some big-ticket items along with the cheapies to encourage students to practice long-term planning in saving up their tickets.

What about taking tickets away from students?

During my years doing behavior modification with students on the spectrum and with ADHD, my mentor in applied behavior analysis (ABA) taught me that we really shouldn't take away rewards already given for positive behavior. If students earn a ticket, they should get to feel the full benefit of it in order for the reinforcement of the behavior to be fully effective. It doesn't make sense to take that same ticket away for a subsequent misbehavior. That sends the message that a slip up totally negates the positive behavior they did earlier. I don't believe this is a helpful message to send—that if your behavior is not perfect all the time, it doesn't matter what strides you make.

> And by the way, keeping a student with ADHD inside for recess as a punishment or sitting the student on the bench during outdoor time doesn't make any sense; these students need to run around outside and get their bodies moving to feel regulated! If you sit them for recess, they will feel that much more antsy when they're back in class.

Over the years, I have taken away plenty of tickets. I wish I hadn't. I was acting impulsively, and even if it helped stop an impulsive behavior in the moment, I don't think it was worth the message it sent in the long run. If a teacher takes away too many tickets, either at once or consistently, students tend to lose engagement with the whole ticket system entirely because it appears to be a game they can't win. They'd rather give up than lose. And then you'd have to think of a whole new reward system just for this student.

Instead of taking away class currency, remind students how they have earned tickets in the past and how they are indeed capable of controlling their impulses and making different choices. Explain that when they're showing a misbehavior, they are missing the chance to earn tickets. But also emphasize that there are plenty of opportunities during the day to earn more.

Keep in mind that for some students with ADHD, outside rewards and consequences are just not effective. Their cognitive, developmental, and executive function challenges make it incredibly difficult for them to enact self-control and inhibit impulses. To withhold rewards from students week after week while rewarding everyone around them will only hurt their self-esteem.

In these cases, find the positive behaviors they are already doing. It could be something small—throwing out their trash after lunch, clearing their desk at the end of the day, handing in a homework assignment. Whatever it is, give them verbal praise and a ticket or whatever, and remind them they are capable of other things, too, like keeping hands to themselves or staying quiet during lessons. Help them start pushing that boulder up the hill by giving them some positive reinforcement for the amount they can already push.

Show Students That Mistakes Are Okay

No one likes making mistakes. This goes for kids as well as adults. Perhaps we believe it makes us look foolish, and so it hurts our self-esteem.

You've probably noticed that some students participate and raise their hands consistently while others never do. Kids who speak out in class are confident. They don't mind making mistakes because if they do, they have enough confidence stored up to withstand the minor blow. Students who don't speak in class may be scared that their mistake will just confirm what they already believe—that they're not smart enough. We have to change their minds about mistakes, or they'll never take any risks in class.

Here's an easy technique that can help.

The next time you happen to make a mistake, don't brush it under the rug. Instead, call attention to it.

Maybe you miscalculate a multiplication problem. Maybe you spell "relevent" wrong (the correct spelling is "relevant"). Perhaps you mix up the date of Pearl Harbor or forget that Olympia, not Seattle, is the capital of Washington. If you admit the error, correct yourself, and show through your demeanor and voice that the mistake is no big deal, your students may believe that to be true. This is incredibly simple and may be effective in easing some stress for those students. Melanie Rothschild discusses in her book *The Art of Mistakes* how becoming comfortable with making mistakes can be an integral part of developing creative muscles, regardless of the discipline, and how our fear of mistakes can hold us back from advancing our own creativity. I have used her book to defend to my students the idea that some mistakes are not only okay, they can result in our coming up with new, innovative ideas.

In the opposite sense, when students see teachers who are perfectionists, who either won't admit to making a mistake or show frustration when it happens, it may add pressure to the room. Perfectionism doesn't mesh well with students with ADHD, since impulsivity and inattentiveness are inevitably going to result in errors. If these students are scared of making mistakes, they're probably going to be reluctant to try any new procedure or project.

Sometimes we have students who really get frustrated when they make mistakes or appear hesitant to participate for fear of failure. For students like these, I've even made mistakes on purpose to show them it's not the end of the world.

To be clear, you don't want to appear unprepared or possessing false knowledge about topics you're teaching. There are certainly times and situations where mistakes can have consequences, and we don't want to promote being misinformed about serious topics. So don't go putting Lincoln on the side of the Confederates or mistaking which countries made up the Axis powers in World War II. Make a small mistake. Maybe you make a spelling error with a strange word or a computational error that could happen to any of us if we're rushing. Maybe you forget a little detail from two chapters ago in the novel you're reading.

Of course, we want students to be accurate in their knowledge and the work they produce. But showing them it's okay to slip up, make a blunder, or misunderstand something may help relieve some of their stress when it does happen to them and also free them up to accept help and correction.

Offer Encouragement and Praise Like Coaches Do

You may have noticed that your students seem to adore and respect anyone they call "Coach." It might be the PE coach, their after-school program coach, their debate coach, or their soccer coach. These people lead activities that the kids love and choose to do. But I think there's another reason why coaches may be effective in motivating students.

Students know that the coaches are playing on the same team as them. Coach Antonio gives lots of verbal encouragement. Coach Andrea gives lots of high fives. Coach Ryan gives fist bumps. Students don't have to call you "Coach," but they should know you're on their team. Praise and gestures like high fives are an easy way to make that clear to students. It also shows that you're proud of them when they achieve success, no matter how small.

Of course, we have to be mindful and methodical about how we offer praise. Token phrases like "Way to go!" or "Nice job!" or "Fantastic!" can come across as empty praise. When phrases like this are offered constantly to a student, they lose meaning and power. It's especially natural in kindergarten to just say "Great job!" or "Great work!" but these phrases don't let students know what specific actions they took to earn the praise, so it doesn't really reinforce behavior or success in a meaningful way.

Instead, it is important to specify to students the exact actions or qualities for which we're praising them. If you are trying to boost their writing confidence, point out a specific sentence they wrote or highlight the correct grammar or an adjective they used for the first time. I often praise students or thank them specifically if they do or say something particularly polite, for example, when they ask me how I'm doing or hold the door open for another student. If you see students really trying to work out a problem in math, you can say, "I

can see how hard you're concentrating right now." At that moment, whether they get it right or wrong isn't as important as their engagement and sustained mental energy.

For some students, hearing words of praise from a teacher means more to them than tangible rewards. It can be hard to decipher which sorts of reinforcements work for a particular student, but here's the thing about verbal praise and high fives:

They're all free and they're super easy to deliver!

ATTENTION GRABBER
We Got This!

Years ago, I sat down with a friend who was advising me about app design and marketing analytics. This was before the social media explosion, before many people were even talking about apps. The stuff was way out of my league. There was a lot of explanation going on, and for sure, my own ability to attend to my friend's teaching was straining like a rubber band pulled to its limit. But there was one thing that really kept me engaged. Every couple of minutes, I would attempt to repeat back to my friend with my own words what he was teaching me.

Every time I attempted to phrase in my own words what he was telling me, I felt foolish. He was so articulate and knowledgeable, and I must have sounded like I was trying to speak a new language.

Of course, he didn't make fun of me.

He would simply say, "You got it." And he wouldn't just say it flatly. He would say . . .

"*Yoooou* got it."

He would draw out that "You" just a little bit to give it emphasis.

This may sound silly, but I could literally feel my confidence growing each time he said it. I've been using that phrase with my students ever since.

   And not only that phrase. I remember one of my students had an affinity for Spanish, so when she finished her work, I'd say, "Fantastico!" She'd repeat it back to me as if this was our battle cry. Another would say "I got this" after I explained something to him, sounding like he was pumping himself up, giving himself confidence. So, if I ever felt like he needed a little extra confidence boost during a difficult task, I would pepper in "You got this." Sometimes, he would repeat it back to me: "I got this."

The Big Takeaway

For our students with attention challenges, confidence and self-esteem can be influential factors on their input and production abilities in the classroom and elsewhere. Confidence and success have a reciprocal relationship. If you have one, the other tends to follow.

For students who don't have either, we can create conditions that result in their attaining one or the other. Setting realistic goals that they can meet independently gives them the opportunity to feel successful. When we give students the chance to show off their strengths, they see that others recognize what they have to offer. Class currencies like tickets or marble jars can reinforce appropriate behavior and impulse control, but they also help a student feel successful.

> Confidence and success have a reciprocal relationship. If you have one, the other tends to follow. For students who don't have either, create conditions that result in their attaining one or the other.

Specific, meaningful verbal praise can boost a student's self-esteem. All of these simple steps help create a positive environment that minimizes stress and failure and promotes confidence.

If our students feel like they can succeed, they are more apt to engage. If they feel like making mistakes is okay, they are more apt to take risks and participate.

You can be a teacher *and* a coach.

Lob your students slow pitches so they can knock 'em out of the park, and then gradually increase the speed. Give high fives. Thumbs ups. Have a pep rally every once in a while to celebrate students' victories.

Every day is a new opportunity for them to feel like champions.

CHAPTER 3

LET OUT THE FIZZ
How to Include Effective Fidgeting and Movement in Class

Let's talk fidgeting.

As teachers, we're aware of sensory processing issues through our students' fidgeting. We know that some kids just need to touch things, possibly in order to satisfy some sort of sensory need or calm their anxiety, and others can't seem to stop their bodies from moving. When we look around classrooms, we see students lifting up their knees to their chests and rocking. We see students playing extended drum solos with their pencils. Tapping their feet. Wiggling in their seats. Running their fingers atop the surface of their desks. Slouching so that their backs are nearly parallel to the floor. Bouncing up and down like a pogo stick. You might notice that your students with ADHD or other attention challenges tend to fidget more often.

Sensory processing is a complex function of the nervous system by which we input and process information through our senses. A person may be under-responsive to sensory stimuli and therefore may seek out more stimuli to feel regulated. One may also be hyper-responsive. In this case, the person tends to avoid too much sensory stimulation because sounds, tastes, smells, and tactile sensations are overwhelming. Occupational therapists are often consulted for students with significant sensory processing issues like these.

> Fidgeting becomes a problem when students attempt to regulate their sensory needs in ways that *add* to their distraction. In other words, they're not fidgeting properly!

Fidgeting becomes a problem in the classroom when students attempt to regulate their sensory needs in ways that *add* to their distraction. On top of that, their fidgeting may be distracting other students, or even you. In other words, they're not fidgeting properly!

I know I fidget sometimes. It happens more noticeably when I'm stressed. If I'm in a tense conversation, I scratch my beard a lot. When I'm under pressure, I'm more sensitive to how tight my belt is; I need it secure, but if it's too tight I feel like I'm being squeezed to death. Sometimes I tap my foot while I'm waiting in line. If I'm taking any sort of exam, I need to twirl the pencil across my fingers rhythmically. This sort of fidgeting calms me down and helps me maintain focus.

I think all adults and kids have sensory needs of some sort. It's just that some people are needier than others.

And on top of students' sensory needs, we're also asking students to sit for the majority of the day. They're bursting with energy on the inside, doing everything they can to contain it. It's no wonder they can't focus on you or their work for very long. Having to sit still for long stretches of time, they're like sealed soda cans that have been shaken up.

We have to figure out ways to let out some of that fizz. And we have to do it in a way that results in more engagement, not more distraction. Some schools and teachers are having occupational therapists come directly to classrooms to observe and give recommendations. But what tools and strategies can we teachers use on our own?

Let's go through the specific sensory-seeking needs and some possible solutions.

Sensory Need: Hands

Thanks to a certain spinning toy that became a cultural phenomenon, the word *fidget* as a noun is now in our public lexicon. But a fidget can be any little object that kids can have in their hands to touch and manipulate to satisfy their sensory needs during class.

Fidgets have the potential to help fulfill students' sensory-seeking needs and help them put more mental energy into lessons and work, but only if they're using the appropriate fidget.

Choose the Right Fidgets

There are several important factors to consider when trying to find fidgets to help with a student's sensory needs. Think of it like matching up a kid with a pet; it has to be the right animal that suits the owner.

Make sure fidgets are tactically satisfying.
Every object we hold in our hands has a
unique tactile quality. Maybe it's smooth and
firm. It might be rough, spiky, or squishy.
Perhaps it has weight to it, or it could be light
and flexible. Whether a student likes pressing
an eraser in between her fingers, squeezing a
squishy ball, or lightly tapping a ruler on the
back of her hand, that student is satisfying a
specific sensory need.

I once had a student who loved flick-
ing through the pages of sticky notes. I
imagine the sensation of the paper flap-
ping on his hands gave him the sort of
input he needed to calm himself.

Often, trial and error is necessary
to see if a particular fidget works for a
student. Have students try out different ones. Observe and figure
out which ones add distraction and which ones satisfy the needs, so
students can focus on your teaching.

Make sure fidgets aren't mentally stimulating. Sometimes a fidget
draws more of a student's attention away from the class.

In the past couple years, different fidget products have exploded
onto the market, but it's important to choose an object that students
are able to manipulate with their hands but not focus on it with their
minds. One reason a fidget may not work is if it's visually appealing
or has too many playful components. When the fidget is so cool-
looking that a student can't help but focus on it and play with it, it's
no longer a fidget—it's a toy. Another issue with some fidgets is that
they become games to the student, or students use them more like

action figures, flying them through the
air or smashing them against things.
Obviously, this issue becomes more
prevalent for younger students; for
kindergartners, it is especially challenging to find fidget items that won't
totally consume their attention.

Ultimately, what we're looking for
in a fidget is an object that satisfies a
specific tactile sensory need but is not
compelling.

A bracelet is an example of a fidget
item that I've seen work on several
occasions. Of course, a charm bracelet
would be distracting; I'm talking about
bracelets without flair that have a
simple design, such as the single-
colored wristbands that usually stand
for a cause like cancer awareness or
that might be advertising a business.
They're simple, have a smooth rubbery
feel, and might serve as a nice, accessible fidget. There are even bracelets on
the market—made with different materials and textures—specifically
designed to satisfy sensory needs. One example is the spiraled rubber
bracelets that look like phone cords from the 1980s. Oftentimes when
kids wear bracelets like these, or typical threaded friendship bracelets, it gives them something to touch that isn't all that interesting.
How long can a bracelet really hold your interest, especially when it's
on you all day? Also, just the feeling of the material on a kid's wrist

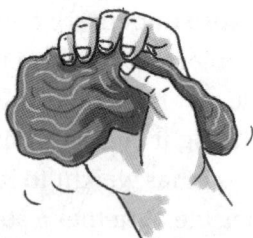

might satisfy some of that sensory-seeking need, and there's little worry that the fidget will fall on the floor and add more distraction.

Give Students Responsibility for Their Fidgets

Chapter 7 has more about self-management, but here is a perfect opportunity to start instilling in your students responsibility for their own supports.

The first step in building responsibility is to make students aware of sensory needs and convey that everyone has them. For younger students, here's a fun way to do this:

Start with a quick lesson about fidgets: What are they? How can they help us? (Or distract us?)

Introduce your students to potential items: sticky notes, erasers, squeeze balls, magnets, wrist bracelets, finger bands, putty, string, and so on. Talk about the ways that some fidgets can help our focus while others do just the opposite. Let kids try out different fidgets to see if any work for them. Discussing fidgets helps students develop awareness of their sensory needs.

Doing a whole lesson about fidgets may feel childish to older students. Instead, just have a quick conversation with them during a break or before class. Explain to them the purpose of fidgets—share your own sensory needs and any fidgeting you may do yourself—and then encourage them to explore fidget items on their own at home, test them out, see what they think might work for them.

Once students find a fidget that suits their needs—and they may need a couple options to have, since their sensory needs may change over the course of a day—they should keep it handy and make sure it doesn't get lost. You'll have to judge if your students are ready for this responsibility. Kindergartners may not be, so you will have to manage the fidget inventory, but your first and second graders might be. If you feel they can do it, empower them to find a safe spot—pencil case, desk, backpack—where they will remember to retrieve the fidget when needed and return it after use. Kids can also be empowered to decide for themselves *when* they need it. For example, if literature circles are a particularly stressful time for a student who often makes a lot of noise by tapping a pencil, remind the student before lit circles begin to grab the fidget. After a couple of days, explain that the student should grab the fidget, along with a copy of the book, before every literature circle. Phase out the reminders and reinforce the student with some verbal praise for doing it independently.

Here's something I once observed that really took me by surprise.

ATTENTION GRABBER
Watch and Learn

Jordan was a third-grade student and technology maven who had some general anxiety and difficulty sustaining mental energy. One morning, he came into class with a big smartwatch on his wrist, a device that has digital games and makes all sorts of noise—a toy if I ever saw one. I told him that the first time the watch became distracting during class, it would have to go in his backpack. I assumed this outcome would arrive in a minute or two.

It didn't. Quite the opposite.

He immediately powered down the watch so it was just a weight around his wrist. I noticed during the day he was more attentive and less fidgety in his seat. Over the ensuing weeks, I witnessed this boy being responsible with this watch in a way I hadn't seen from him before. He took it off while playing sports and put it somewhere safe. He asked politely for help to put it back on. He made sure the watch was powered down during the school day so it didn't make noise. It was like a pet he had to take care of, and he rose to the occasion.

I believe he took such good care of it because it was something he felt invested in. Again, technology was his thing, so if he did lose track of it or was made to put it away, he could foresee that he would be devastated. It's often hard to get students with attention challenges to see steps ahead like this in order to take care of belongings, but if it's something they truly care about, they can more easily show responsibility. (Keeping track of materials is addressed further in chapter 7.)

And from my observation, the feeling of the watch on his wrist satisfied some of his hand's sensory needs and lowered his anxiety.

Another problem that can arise is that fidgets can become projectiles. Students may drop them on the floor or "accidentally" flick them or even fire them across the room. We don't want our classroom turning into a game of dodgeball! For these students, you can try a fidget that is stationary. For example, you can put a small strip of Velcro either on top or underneath the desk so students can easily rub their hands and fingers across it. You could also tape down other materials like something fuzzy or smooth, depending on what sort of tactile sensation the student prefers.

If students really do need a particular fidget that you just can't fasten down, this is another opportunity to speak with students about responsibility. Explain to them that the fidget is there to help, but if it leaves their hands and becomes distracting to themselves or other people, it no longer has a purpose. Convey trust in them that they will take care of the item and use it appropriately.

This doesn't work every time, of course. Sometimes you have to take away a fidget, at least for the duration of the lesson. Take a few moments after class to discuss the situation with the student and work together to figure out an alternative fidget solution.

Sensory Need: Legs, Feet, and Seat

Oh those kicking, swinging, tapping, noise-making feet. Sometimes it sounds like you're teaching a tap dancing class, no? If you simply tell your students to stop, they might stop for a few minutes, but this doesn't eliminate their need to seek sensory input with their feet. You may have stopped the noise, but their anxiety could rise.

Keep Feet Grounded

If you're teaching in the early grades, you might notice a Broadway chorus line of swinging legs under the tables. Here's the first thing to consider: When students sit naturally, are their feet touching the ground?

ATTENTION GRABBER
Foot Rest Remedy

I had a first-grade student who could not sit comfortably in his chair. His legs and feet flailed around like tentacles. Half the time, his body would be sideways, and when he was really feeling antsy he'd end up on the floor. An occupational therapist observed him and said, "His feet aren't touching the floor, and he doesn't feel grounded. Get him a stool to put his feet on."

Mind.

Blown.

Throughout the rest of the day, I observed him further and noticed that he would often fold his legs up under himself, sitting crisscross applesauce on his chair, or he

would put his feet inside his desk. It appeared that he was doing anything he could to avoid having his feet dangling above the floor.

Kids' legs can be like lightning bolts. Until they reach a destination, they're erratic, full of electricity, in search of a stable object to strike.

I got him the stool the next day, put it under his desk, and *bam*—instant improvement.

At times he'd say he didn't need it, and I would put it away and tell him he could just grab it when he did need it. And that is exactly what he proceeded to do. That is self-management. There were times when he'd knock over the stool on its side, sometimes purposefully, and I would have to speak with him about being responsible with it. Or, perhaps, this was a signal that he needed to stand up for a minute and shake out his legs.

Use Elastic Bands

Here's another support that's gaining popularity in classrooms: elastic bands on the front legs of all the chairs. These bands are stretchy and allow kids to bounce, rest, and press their feet against them to feel resistance. The bands don't make noise, and they don't take up space.

Many teachers have told me these bands can be extremely effective in curbing leg fidgeting and increasing student engagement.

Offer Alternative Seating

Consider this: Anyone who works in an office seven hours a day needs a comfortable chair, one with a soft seat, wheels on the floor for flexibility, and back support.

I'm not implying we buy cushioned rolling chairs for our students. I'm only suggesting that maybe their seats don't exactly feel like massage chairs. For students with significant difficulties with sitting, you can get blow-up cushions specifically designed to satisfy sensory needs. These go on the seat and often have some sort of tactile feature: bumps, ridges, anything to provide that extra sensory input.

Kindergartners are often being asked to sit on the floor, and the rainbow-colored carpet isn't as cushy as we think it is. Hence, the nonstop wiggling and distraction! There are all sorts of cushions made for floor use, and these might help young students find comfort during carpet-time. It can be tough to let only one or two of your kindergartners use an alternative seat, so you could rotate use of the cushions if you only have a few. Better yet, talk to your administration about buying them for the whole class.

Of course, cushions are mainly for primary-grade students; middle schoolers probably don't want to be seen using a squishy seat support. But you could encourage them to throw down a nicely folded sweatshirt to sit on or perhaps even keep some folded-up blankets in the room for a student who might benefit from sitting on one. Or have them take responsibility for their own sensory needs and bring one from home.

Cushions are not the only type of alternative seating you can use. In a study conducted with fourth and fifth graders, students with ADHD-like symptoms experienced increased levels of attention and decreased hyperactivity while seated on stability balls in classrooms.[4] Some teachers incorporate alternative seating into their classrooms in a big way. They've brought in yoga balls, flexible sitting stools, and even beanbag chairs for certain activities. I once saw a teacher who rotates the different seats among the students so all the kids get the opportunity to use each option.

Sensory Need: Whole Body

There has been a lot of interest in and research on exploring how bringing physical activity into classrooms during lessons may improve time-on-task and general academic outcomes. Studies have shown that aerobic exercise at a moderate to vigorous intensity appears to promote children's effortful and goal-directed cognition.[5] The physical activity stimulates chemicals in the brain that can prompt our executive functions. Entire programs have even been developed that integrate physical activity into lessons, and certainly

While many students are more attentive while seated, some think better on their feet . . . literally. Have ways to get these students up and moving that do not disrupt others.

these are worth exploring. But if you don't have the resources for a program, or if you want to implement something on the fly, you can find lots of quick ways to bring physical movement into your classroom during lessons.

While many students are more attentive while seated, it certainly is not true for all of them. There are those who think better on their feet . . . literally. It's helpful to have quick ways to get these students up and moving, but in a way that does not disrupt others. Give students a few more opportunities during class, aside from break times, to release some of that fizz.

Get Them Up to the Board

Come on down! You're the next contestant on *The Price Is Right!*

When a student gets called up to the front and gets to write on the board or point something out or even just stand at the front of the room, they immediately become more involved. How could they not? They're standing right in front of you and the whole class. If you make calling up students a regular routine, they will be anticipating their turn. And that anticipation is something that might influence their attention to your lesson.

A crucial point here:

I once made the mistake of calling up a student who was absolutely horrified to be in front of the class. It was quickly evident from the expression on his face and squirmy body language. In retrospect, he was probably scared of failing in front of his peers. We need to be ultrasensitive to this. You can still call these students up to the board; just be sure they can do whatever you're asking them to do. For these kids, the result of calling them up could be that much greater. Not only are they succeeding, they're succeeding in front of everybody. Again, confidence can result in further participation from students.

Another crucial point is that teenagers often hate having the spotlight on them. I would avoid calling up middle school students individually to the board. However, you could call up five students to do math problems on the board, or any sort of written work, and another five could stand next to them and check their work for errors. That makes ten kids being on their feet, participating, while the other students are anticipating their turns. This helps get the whole class involved at once without singling out any particular person.

Have Them Act It Out

Young people are natural actors, and most of them love to act. Let's capitalize on that tool. The narrative qualities of history and literature make using scripts and acting a natural fit. When students act out famous influential figures or powerful scenes from novels, they are engaging with class content in a way that encourages their creativity and movement. For example, many teachers turn biography reports into "living museum" projects where students dress up as historical figures. These sorts of activities can be simplified and sprinkled into lessons.

If you're teaching about the government, divide students into the three branches and try to pass a new law. If you're studying colonial times, you could start by having students act out how it must have felt to be on the *Mayflower* or the other ships coming over from England. If you're reading *Holes*, you could have students act out laboring in the desert, nearly fainting of thirst. Younger kids especially love getting out of their seats to act. You could have them do something as simple as playing charades to learn new verbs or having them form their arms and legs into letters, YMCA-style.

And, like the "living museum" project, you can also make a bigger production that's fun for you and the students.

ATTENTION GRABBER
Poseidon for President!

Shooting and editing video is one of my hobbies, and I've enjoyed integrating it into the classroom. I used to offer my video skills at a school serving twice-exceptional students, working with human- ities teachers to produce curriculum-based videos with the students as writers and actors. Twice-exceptional students typically are very creative, but their learning challenges combined with executive func- tioning issues often make it extremely difficult for them to produce work and participate. To help with engagement, the humanities teachers would write scripts with their students as a final group proj- ect for whatever unit they were studying.

In a sixth-grade class that had been studying Greek mythology, the teacher told me that some of the students had a lot of difficulty speaking out in class, with some of them rarely participating: one student had a stutter that made verbal expression extremely chal- lenging, another girl was very reserved.

The students had written a short play depicting some of the Greek gods on a political talk show. Each of the gods had to make a case for why he or she should be "president" of Mt. Olympus. It was quite brilliant, actually. Along with key pieces of information about the mythology itself, students also worked in some political satire. The teacher had spent a lot of time prepping with the kids, having them rehearse their lines, and they even brought in costumes.

Honestly, I didn't have to do much direction at all. By the time I got there to start filming, the students were ready to perform. It was amazing to see them act out the characters of Ares, Zeus, Athena, and others, including an old-timey news interviewer. They were all so enthusiastic about performing! Even the girl who was usually shy performed like a pro.

I edited the video together, and students got to see themselves bring the course content to life. This was years ago, so video editing was a bit more complicated, but now everyone has a camera on their phones and user-friendly editing software usually comes with computers, so it's much easier to make little movies in class.

That said, making the movie was just icing on the cake. The important attention grabber was the play itself. Students who rarely participated in class suddenly wanted to join in and play pretend. They were clearly more engaged by performing than they'd been with the material just speaking about it in class. The student who stuttered got through his lines and gave a fantastic performance as Zeus, and the girl who was reserved went on to participate in the school's drama program.

What about math? You are dealing with numbers and operations that most easily lend themselves to representations on the page—hence, worksheets and workbooks—so it's much more difficult to find natural uses for the performance tool. It takes a bit more thought, but when you find ways to incorporate acting into math, it can be that much more engaging because the students don't expect it.

ATTENTION GRABBER
To Borrow or Not to Borrow?

I was a resource specialist teacher supporting some students in a second-grade class, and the lead teacher and I were attempting to teach multi-digit subtraction with regrouping, or "borrowing," to a group of students with attention deficits. Due to this procedure having four thousand steps, our kids were having difficulty mustering the mental energy required. We were working on the problem 64–37, and the students were looking everywhere except at the whiteboard. The lead teacher called Elijah and Nina to the front of the room. As the teacher began narrating a "borrowing" story—saying, "Elijah and Nina are the number 64 and they need to subtract 37 from themselves"—I quickly handed them each a whiteboard to hold in front of them.

The two students each wrote a number on their board that corresponded to a digit in 64. Elijah was 4 and Nina was 6. Elijah was asked to subtract 7 (the ones digit of 37) from his own 4. Of course, because 7 is greater than 4, it couldn't be done, so he had to go "borrow" from his neighbor Nina, who was stationed outside the classroom door. Elijah went over to the door and knocked. Nina opened the door and improvised.

Nina: "Yes, may I help you?"

Elijah: "I don't have enough to subtract 7 from me, so may I borrow a ten, please?"

Nina: "Sure, dahling."

Nina said this with a mid-Atlantic, old Hollywood accent. Where do kids get this stuff? Elijah then added the 10 to the number on his board and changed it to 14. Nina changed her number to 5.

Borrowing! Regrouping!

Acting!

In the ensuing days, students were more attentive, asking frequently if they could be next to act out the math scene. They also appeared to enjoy seeing their classmates' different artistic interpretations of the scene. Who would win the Academy Award for best performance in a math problem?

Using any sort of hands-on materials for math may help engage students, whether it's colorful counting cubes, pizza cutouts for fractions, fake money, place value flipcharts, place value blocks, or mini-clocks. Here's a story that combines acting with a more hands-on approach.

ATTENTION GRABBER
Semisweet Multiplication

In the same classroom as the borrowing "story," the teacher and I were teaching our attention-challenged students how to draw pictures to represent multiplication. For 3 x 5, we drew three circles on the board and then drew five stars in each circle. We instructed the students to do their own problems on whiteboards, which worked for many of our kids. However, one of our students with severe attention challenges would take minutes to draw one circle because she repeatedly drew a messy circle and tried to make it neater . . . but she just couldn't. Another student would draw the stars inside the circles so sloppily that he couldn't tell how many stars were in there. These are output control issues, specifically graphomotor and visual-motor difficulties, and in this case, they make any sort of handwriting, including on whiteboards, very challenging. And there were other students who were simply having difficulty with the concepts.

To take handwriting out of the equation, my co-teacher and I made a plan to get students on their feet. We decided that we would turn our classroom into a bakery and have students act out being cookie bakers.

In preparation for the next day, we cut out some circles on beige construction paper to make cookie shapes and spent two bucks on a bag of semisweet chocolate chips. We divided the kids into four baking teams and gave each team some paper cookies and a cup full of chocolate chips. Then we put a word problem on the board and instructed groups to bake cookies for six party guests—six cookies, each of which must have seven chocolate chips.

You can imagine the looks of glee on their faces as they poured chips out onto the napkins on their tables. We looked around and saw all of the students having fun with the activity, figuring out how to distribute the chocolate chips. Manipulating the chips was easier for those students with graphomotor issues who were struggling with the whiteboards.

After the groups were finished, we asked them how many chocolate chips they needed. All of the groups had the same answer. We wrote the corresponding multiplication sentence on the board and drew a matching picture with circles and stars.

Next round, we just put a number sentence on the board and made it into a contest: Which group can bake the fastest?

$$6 \times 7 = 42$$

Putting chips onto a paper cookie removed the production control issues our students were having with the whiteboards. All of the mental energy they would have spent just trying to draw one

CHAPTER 3 Let Out the Fizz: How to Include Effective Fidgeting and Movement in Class   79

circle became available to actually figure out the problem using the cookies and chips.

And of course, we all had a little chocolate chip dessert before recess.

Make Math on the Move

Aside from acting, there are other ways to get students moving to help with their engagement with math. If you're teaching any sort of geometry, students with visual-motor integration or fine motor challenges may have difficulty using the necessary skills to figure out problems. Geometry requires being able to see shapes, lines, and angles clearly, and often requires using a pencil to trace along lines.

To increase the involvement of students who may be struggling, get students out of their seats by having them use masking tape to build shapes, grids, or intersecting lines on the floor. For example, if you're studying parallelograms, guide students to form large ones on the floor using tape. Encourage students to think about the qualities of the shape and then roll out the tape to make the lines. This could also apply to geometry at the secondary level when students learn formulas regarding triangles, the sizes of angles, and even coordinate grids. If you have students with gross motor challenges, pair them up with other students who can work with them as a team to complete the task.

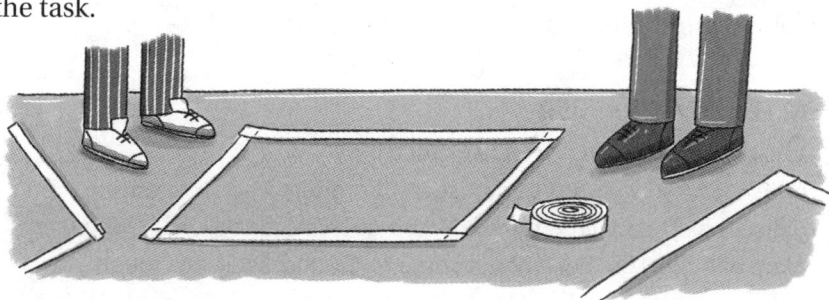

Instead of having to sit in their seat and rely strictly on their input controls, students can be physically active in the learning process, making shapes and angles that they can stand on, walk across, and engage with.

Another way to incorporate movement into math is to use hand and arm motions. For students with attention challenges, remembering complex or multistep operations can be terribly difficult. One student in particular, Deana, struggled greatly with basic subtraction because she would include the original number when starting to count down. For example, for 9–4, she would start with 9 and count down *four* places to arrive at an answer of 6: "Nine, eight, seven, six." She had an educational therapist working with her who understood she learned better kinesthetically when her body was moving, so the ET taught her to tap her head once lightly when saying the original number and then start counting down while using fingers to track the amount. In other words, she gently tapped her head while saying "nine" and then began counting down "eight, seven, six" while raising fingers. This prevented her from starting her countdown on the 9 itself.

Another example is having the student "karate chop" a number when doing division. Or, when teaching how to cross-multiply to solve algebraic equations with fractions, have students make an *X* with their crossed arms in the air. This sums up the main idea, gets the blood pumping, and it's fun.

ATTENTION GRABBER
Skip-Counting Hopscotch

I once worked with a group of second graders who were having difficulty skip-counting, primarily with counting backward. They were okay with the 10s, but when it came to 2s and 5s, it was tough for them to mentally make the jumps. On top of that, these were students who typically used fidgets and were often seeking sensory input. I always keep chalk handy, so I grabbed some and took the students outside.

Just outside the classroom, I quickly drew ten boxes in a row on the pavement in the shape of a hopscotch court. I wrote numbers inside the boxes, labeling them by 5s up through 50. I found a rock on the ground and modeled for them a new kind of hopscotch. I threw the rock, and it landed on the 45. I picked up the rock, stood on the 45 square, and hopped backward while counting down by fives: 40, 35, 30, 25, and so on.

Immediately, the students were all raising their hands, pleading to be picked to go next. This was great: I had their attention. But when I chose the next student, and he began jumping, I noticed the others began attending to other things in the yard behind us—notably, the serious construction going on for the remodeling of the school cafeteria. I was about to take them back inside, but instead, I tried another tactic.

To turn their attention back to me, I told my students that in choosing who would take a turn next, I would only select from students who counted along with the current jumper. This incentive alone helped students ignore the stimuli behind us and focus on the math.

Everyone took a turn jumping and skip-counting backward, and the next day, I repeated this activity with 2s.

Any time you take students with attention challenges outside for an activity, they might instinctively start bouncing or drifting away, or they may become more interested in whatever's going on outside. In this case, there was an incredible amount of noise and building in the background. However, if your activity keeps them active and participating, it will take precedence for them over anything else.

Let Them Stand (and Deliver)

Yes, that's a reference to the amazing movie about calculus teacher extraordinaire Jaime Escalante. But it's also a reminder to us. If a student would rather stand behind her chair during a lesson, and it's clear that she listens better and stays more alert this way, why not allow it? I once worked in a fourth-grade class where the most intellectually gifted student was given this privilege by the teacher. He just couldn't bear to sit in a seat for long periods. He would even wander across the back of the room, not bothering anybody or making any noise while remaining attentive to lessons.

Sometimes, though, the student you allow to do this *does* start jumping around or making noises or distracting other students. This has happened to me. I learned that before you grant the privilege of standing during class, you have to set rules. Number one, no disrupting other students. Number two, if it does not help the student participate in lessons, then the deal is off. I've found that students often respond when you ask them to be responsible with something specific, even with students who normally seem out of control with their bodies. They deserve opportunities to practice this sort of self-management, and even if they fail to control themselves, we can use the opportunity to start growing their awareness of their own sensory needs.

I've never seen a class where more than three students actually prefer standing while learning. But for those two or three kids who benefit, it's a simple accommodation that costs neither a cent nor a moment of planning.

Let Them Shake, Shake It Off

In between direct instruction and independent work time, give students a brain break. Get them on their feet and do some stretches.

Let them run in place. You don't need to turn your room into a gym, just a place where students can wiggle around for a minute. Or take them outside for two minutes and run them around the yard. Lead them in some jumping jacks. Make it into a contest. Take them for a walk. Go look at some trees. Whatever. As long as they're moving.

When I'm attending a lecture or seminar, I have to get up every thirty minutes or so, or my attentiveness starts to fade. Usually, just a quick stretch or two-minute walk outside will help my mind breathe, and then I'm ready to sit for another thirty minutes of information intake. For that student in the back who really struggles to sustain focus for fifty minutes, find a proper moment in the lesson to encourage her to take a quick walk. Better that she misses two or three minutes of class than is made to sit through fifty straight minutes with her input controls burning out. You can speak with students who may need breaks on a daily basis and empower them to do so independently when they feel it's necessary to replenish their mental energy. You'll want to set parameters beforehand, but in my experience, students don't abuse these breaks. Instead, they use them effectively to help themselves remain engaged.

Another way to keep students active is to assign them a classroom job to be responsible for. Need a note taken to the office? Need help collecting the essays due today? Ask your attention-challenged students to do it. Aside from getting them moving, it also allows them to exercise their input and production abilities, having to follow multistep directions. Giving students little jobs makes them feel capable and trustworthy.

You can even set a designated spot in the classroom so that if a student needs it, he can go back there and shake off some of that excess energy.

GUEST SPEAKER
GIACOMO DELGADO

Giacomo Delgado teaches math and science at the secondary level at a public school. His students have learning and developmental challenges including dyslexia, autism, and social-emotional difficulties. Here he talks about how he uses "scavenger hunts" to engage struggling students.

My students had been working on algebra, which often involves multiple steps and can be very difficult for them. A few students in particular really struggled to be attentive and learn new concepts. I noticed it happening as I was teaching them how to graph linear equalities using the equation $y = mx + b$. Some of my students just couldn't grasp it, and they would tune out.

I often create activities in the classroom that are fun and get students on their feet while also practicing a new concept in a more relaxing format. For example, I'll tape up equations on the walls around the room and do the same with solutions and ask kids to go around the room, pick the equations and solutions off the walls and match them up.

For linear equations, I decided to do something a little bigger. I designed a scavenger hunt that would really get *all* students involved. I divided my students into groups of three. Each member of the group was assigned a job based on what he or she could do best. One would be proficient in linear equations. One would handle finding coordinates. The third would be "the runner." The runners were the students who weren't able to do the math yet, the ones I was really targeting with this activity.

I took an overhead picture of the courtyard in the center of the school campus and put a four-quadrant coordinate grid over it. Each group had this as a map.

The first task was to take a linear equation in standard form (for example, $3x+2y = 2$) and convert it to slope-intercept form ($y = -3/2x + 1$). One of the students who was already good at this took that job. The next student would then plot the y-intercept and use the slope to find two other points on the grid that would make up the line. These first two students would act as teachers and show the third student, the one who was struggling, how they were doing the steps. As "the runner," the third student would take the map with the coordinates and go to the three locations and find a clue that I left.

The runners were excited to go out to the quad with the map and follow the coordinates. I think they really felt part of the team, even though they couldn't do the math yet on their own. The clue they brought back to their team had another linear equation on it, and the team did the cycle again— except this time, they switched jobs. Obviously, the runners needed support from their teammates to do one of the other jobs, but they were participating and open to the process.

You might think scavenger hunts are only for younger students, but it's easy to envision Giacomo's older students being totally into the game he planned for them. Having less-engaged students feel like they're a contributing part of a team and then learning the math from their teammates is a great tool to promote participation and camaraderie. The activity he describes obviously takes some planning, but you can set up simpler versions of games like this in the classroom as well. Maybe even use them as a warm-up when the kids first come in to get them moving immediately.

The Big Takeaway

It can drive you mad trying to teach while kids are fidgeting, tapping, and bouncing. They're not listening to you, and they may be

> Sensory needs are the first things we should attend to. They will probably take precedence for students over anything you have to teach.

distracting others. More importantly, they may be extremely anxious. We need to be proactive. If we just play defense, we'll be taking things out of kids' hands all day and leaving them with no way to satisfy their sensory needs. In a way, sensory needs are the first things we should attend to. They will probably take precedence for students over anything you have to teach.

For starters, figure out what sort of fidgets they can manipulate during lessons that will help them focus. It could be putty they can squeeze, a Velcro strip on their desk, or a flexible bracelet. Be attentive to how they're seated, and see if there's a way to make them more comfortable—maybe a sensory cushion or an alternative seat like a yoga ball.

If left in a natural state, some kids will hop and run and bounce and spin and waddle until they hit a wall. And then they will simply turn direction. They're not meant to be confined to classrooms all day, sitting in chairs. Unfortunately, classrooms aren't going away, and neither is the seven-hour school day. If we want our students to attend better to our teaching, to their work, and to their own behavior, we must keep them physically active in the classroom. This can involve acting or bringing up students to the board. Maybe it's just incorporating some physical movement into math or letting students stand up if they feel antsy.

Every few minutes, get them on their feet and doing something.

CHAPTER 4

SEND THEM IN THE WRITE DIRECTION
How to Promote Writing Production

Writing can be terribly stressful.

How many of us have stared at a computer screen, struggling to find the right words for an email to our boss or a friend or a potential business connection. We not only have to worry if we're getting across our intended meaning, but also if our sentences flow together seamlessly, if our grammar is correct, if we're using the right tone to match the situation. Natural writers have no idea how much stress this causes other people.

Possessing writing ability is empowering, and students who struggle with it may feel powerless, in a sense.

For many students with production issues, writing is their greatest challenge. First off, they must generate ideas. This in itself can be stressful, since this involves considering information already taken in, processing it, and creating an original thought based on that content. This process can use up a lot of a student's mental energy before even trying to form a sentence. To those without attention issues, brainstorming may be done quickly and easily, possibly within minutes. Our affected students may need ten to twenty minutes just to review the prompt and topic and even more time to contemplate their own opinions.

And they haven't yet gotten to the actual printing of words.

The tools in this chapter are geared toward engaging students with the writing process, lowering their anxiety, and increasing their confidence.

Go Beyond the Pencil

Some students with attention deficits rush through their writing impulsively, and their handwriting ends up looking like a Jackson Pollack painting. This might also be the result of graphomotor or visual-motor integration issues; for those students, just gripping a pencil and trying to control it can tire them out. Erasing is a whole other issue. Some students continually make errors and have to erase, and this cycle quickly results in a smattering of erase marks, lead remnants, shredded erasers, and rips and tears all over the paper. All of this uses up students' mental energy.

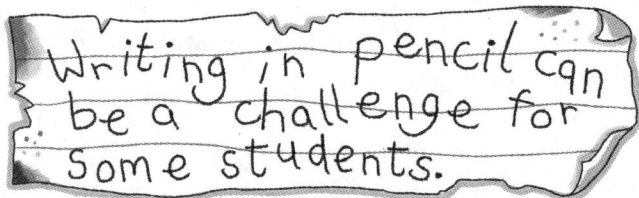

Writing in pencil can be a challenge for some students.

Let's prevent students from making these works of modern art.

Students need to have the writing tool that works for them. For some kids, giving them a pencil to write with is like giving a hammer to someone who needs to dig a hole. It can work technically, maybe, but boy is it going to be exhausting.

I see lots of teachers these days integrating dry-erase whiteboard activities for short assignments and quick activities. Dry-erase markers are bright and colorful, and they make the mechanics of writing easier because the marker tip glides smoothly across the board's surface. It's also easy to quickly erase mistakes. In my experience, dry-erase boards can result in increased production.

> For some kids, giving them a pencil to write with is like giving a hammer to someone who needs to dig a hole. It can work technically, but boy is it going to be exhausting.

A potential pitfall to using these is that many of our students cannot resist doodling on the board instead of working out problems, or they doodle when you're teaching them a new skill. Also, the markers themselves may quickly become fidgets, which may or may not be distracting them from learning.

> Doodling isn't always a distraction for students. I once had a student who would doodle in the margins of his notebook, and it helped him remain mentally present in the classroom and listen to the teacher; he didn't need to look at the teacher to absorb the lesson auditorily. Of course, if there was something relevant on the whiteboard, he would need to pause a moment and look up. The point is that doodling certainly can be beneficial for some students, but if it is preventing them from doing work or from watching you while you're teaching a new math skill or visual concept, it's working against them.

Here are some simple adjustments:

- Don't have students take out the dry-erase marker and whiteboard until your lesson is completed and it's time for them to start trying problems or writing.
- Designate a spot where students put their markers during listening times. Maybe it's in a pencil box or a special cup at the corner of their desks.
- Tell students the rule: If they doodle instead of working, no more dry-erase board.

I also see more teachers having students write with mechanical pencils. They're lightweight, they usually have a built-in rubber grip, and the lead tips are highly sensitive, which could prompt your students with fine motor challenges to be more controlled in their manipulation of the pencil. I've seen this happen; a student who wrote gigantic, messy letters with a normal pencil was suddenly writing more neatly on the lines.

The main issue with mechanical pencils is the reloading. Buying extra lead for the classroom is an expense, for sure, although you could tell the students who want to use them that they have to bring their own refills. On top of that, students often seem preoccupied with changing out the lead, and this can be a distraction. Then again, the constant sharpening of standard pencils produces the same result. You could troubleshoot this by having students check and reload their mechanical pencil every morning as a ritual. This should last them the day, so you can then put a ban on reloading during class time. (If they want to do it at recess, go for it!)

Mechanical pencils may be too distracting for some students, but they can work well in many cases, so they're definitely worth trying.

Set Up Students for Quick Successes

As students get older, we expect longer and longer pieces of writing from them. This is a gradual process of methodically challenging students to dig a little deeper; produce more thoughts, ideas, and sentences; and use more meticulous organization. The reality is that students with challenges may not be ready to produce as much as is expected from the rest of the class. More importantly, the stress of this expectation may affect them in such a way that they'll simply shut down.

As discussed in chapter 2, we can give shorter assignments to these students to help them feel successful and to gain practice producing on the page. There are different ways to accomplish this.

Use Graphic Organizers

Simple prewriting activities that require less actual writing can be great tools for giving students confidence. When students brainstorm for graphic organizers like bubble maps, tree maps, or story maps, to name a few, they are taking a step in the writing process that requires less mental energy but also gives them a sense of moving forward. Before assignments like paragraphs or essays, have students brainstorm ideas and write them on a visual frame and/or create a basic outline.

Brainstorming can even help students as young as kindergarten, who are often tasked with very short writing assignments such as completing a full sentence. If you want young students to write a sentence about what they did yesterday, have them first write a couple of words in bubbles on a bubble map to get them started. Starting with a shorter task often helps students stay engaged right off the bat and can make the task seem more manageable.

ATTENTION GRABBER
Story Map of Ember

When students read novels for class, they are often asked to write reading responses or summaries of chapters as they go through the book. Generally speaking, reading novels is difficult for students with attention challenges, and when they're asked to write about characters or plot as they go, it may feel overwhelming to them because they're already spending so much mental energy dealing with the language and story elements.

One tool I use to promote production from students regarding novels is story maps. My fourth-grade student Evan was just starting to feel confident enough to try reading entire novels independently. One of the first big novels he read was *The City of Ember*. His classroom teacher assigned weekly reading responses, and since I was working with him after school, I supported him in these assignments.

Evan often struggled with sustaining mental energy during any sort of task, so writing production was extremely difficult for him. He expressed that even looking at a blank page made him feel anxious. I knew that writing his own thoughts about a story would be a challenging element for his mind to process. So, before he attempted to write reading responses, I wanted him to engage with writing about a novel in a much simpler and condensed format. I checked out some story maps online, but I ended up making my own in PowerPoint, one I thought would be visually interesting for him. It included different shapes and colored boxes for characters, setting, problem, conflict/action, climax, and resolution.

STORY MAP

3. PROBLEM

- Food: not enough for everyone
- Work: Ember people have to work hard

4. CONFLICT/ADVENTURE

- Lina sneaks on to Casper's cart to go to the city.
- The city is in ruins.
- In Sparks at the plaza, grafitti says Ember people should leave.
- Tick wants to fight Sparks, so he tries to get Ember people fired up.
- Sparks want to kick them out. Sparks has a machine gun, Ben tries to fire gun but it explodes.

5. SOLUTION

Finally, they all join up and work together.

STORY TITLE
People of Sparks

1. CHARACTERS

- Lina
- Doon
- Poppy
- Torren
- Mrs. Murdo
- Tick
- Clary
- Casper

2. SETTING

- Land of Sparks
- Pioneer Hotel
- Dr. Hester's House
- The Plaza

6. RESOLUTION

Doon used the science book to finish his creation and create electricity. Light bulb lights up!

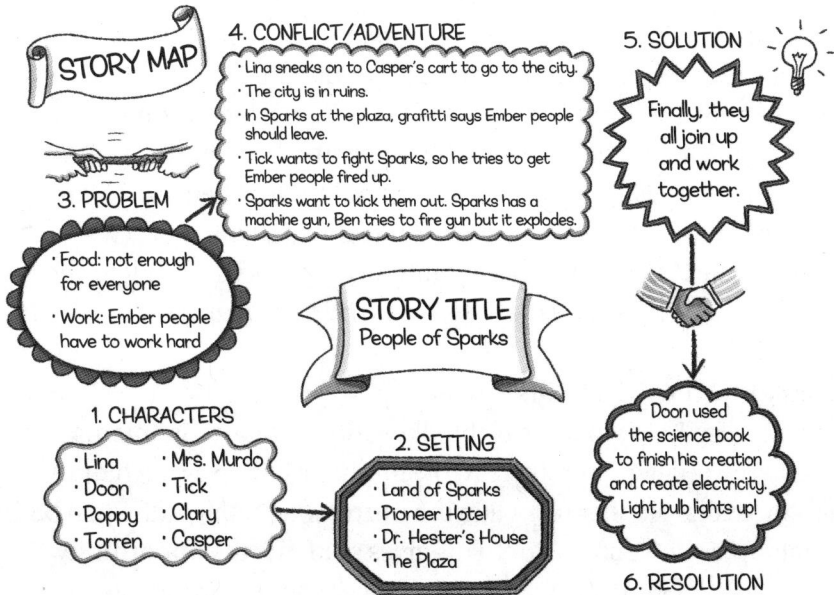

This gave Evan the opportunity to start outputting simple details about the second book in the series, *The People of Sparks*: character names like Lina and Doon and the main places in the story like the Pioneer Hotel, Dr. Hester's house, and the plaza—easy stuff to get him in the flow of typing some information. Then we discussed what he thought about the main problem of the story. He typed into the problem box that there wasn't enough food for everyone and the people of Ember had to work very hard. Next he moved on to the conflict/action section and added plot points.

We used story maps often throughout the year. After warming up to producing these sorts of basic writing tasks, Evan subsequently grew more apt to engage with longer and more complex assignments. His weekly reading responses could entail writing a letter to the author, saying how he would change a story element, or making a prediction. Though his initial responses were short, he gradually grew more comfortable, and his production increased week by week.

When students reach middle school, they're expected to be able to take a writing prompt or task and go through the process of coming up with ideas, writing five paragraphs, and revising to complete a final draft. Often when I meet with older students after school who have huge essays to write, they seem totally overwhelmed. Giving them prewriting tasks like brainstorming ideas, coming up with possible theses, and creating an outline helps them complete shorter stages of writing as they move toward writing paragraphs.

Break Down Assignments

You can also help students by breaking down long assignments into a series of smaller ones. Instead of simply assigning a rough draft, assign several smaller tasks like the introduction, the individual body paragraphs, and conclusion. This gives students the opportunity to tackle smaller chunks of writing at a time. Elementary school teachers often walk their students through this process, but the reality is that some of our middle school students can truly benefit from it as well, with the ultimate goal being that students will learn how to break down their assignments independently.

Shorten Assignments

Shortening assignments for some students can help relieve stress for them and help them gradually build up to the standard you set for the rest of the class. While the rest of the class writes five paragraphs discussing symbolism in *To Kill a Mockingbird*, let your impacted students write three or four. Instead of requiring four quotes from a novel to defend their thesis, make it two or three. Set expectations that make the task appear more manageable to them. Often, when students perceive something is doable, their increased confidence may result in more sustained attention.

The lowering of expectations for assignments might appear to contradict the ideals of increasing rigor and pushing students to think critically and improve writing skills. Some teachers might be uncomfortable lowering the bar for struggling students, fearing that the continually rising standards will leave them behind.

My response to this concern is that by shortening an assignment or starting a student with an easier writing task, we're not handing out a life sentence of lowered expectations. This is a temporary but crucial adjustment. If students struggle with writing production, maintaining rigorous standards of output might stifle them or result in a continual failing to reach goals. A student with attention challenges will probably not see rigorous standards as an opportunity to "try harder." They're already trying as hard as their mental energy will allow. But if they can get a rhythm going, hit some marks—even if they aren't producing as much as their classmates—they may be able to write a bit more next time.

Have Students Type

Books like Trilling and Fadel's *21st Century Skills*[6] consider our rapidly changing world and predict an evolving classroom that adapts to how skills like critical thinking and problem-solving are learned and practiced in everyday life. One of their three main categories of 21st-century skills is digital literacy. Obviously, digital literacy encompasses a broad and complex range of skills, but in my view, the most basic is word processing.

Many of today's high school students are writing their papers on a computer. Some teachers even prefer to be emailed reports and essays rather than receiving a hard copy. More and more teachers are using websites like Turnitin.com that facilitate students and teachers exchanging papers and comments through apps, and every year, it appears more are simply using Google Classroom, Docs, and Slides to streamline the workflow. This is what the 21st-century classroom looks like, and it reflects the way information is shared in the world beyond education.

Research supports the idea that students using word processing produce better quality compositions, and low-achieving students make even greater improvements.[7]

But many elementary and middle school students are still expected to write their paragraphs and essays by hand. If they're going to be typing on computers for the rest of their lives, it makes sense to start them on this interface as early as possible.

Of course, computers and tablets cost money, and maybe your school is struggling just to have working water fountains. If you don't have technology available for your students, speak with your administrators to see what can be done: grants, fundraisers, drives to acquire used equipment, and so on. It's certainly a worthy cause to fight for. Also consider talking with your technology specialist, who may be able to dig up one or more used laptops for little (or no) money. I have been in plenty of situations when technology was not readily available. To compensate, I bring my own laptop and often have students use it for writing projects. If you don't own a laptop, or haven't even considered buying one, they are quite affordable these days; you can usually find one for under $200.

The Office of Educational Technology—part of the Department of Education—put out a National Education Technology Plan called "Reimagining the Role of Technology in Education" in 2016 (updated in 2017). The document contains many organizations and resources meant to help underfunded schools get technology. For example, the Schools and Libraries E-rate Program is a source of federal funding for internet connectivity in US schools and libraries. You can find the document at **tech.ed.gov/files/2017/01/NETP17.pdf**.

Typing is now the dominant form of written communication. With emailing, social media, tweeting, and texting, the amount of typing most of us do far outweighs our handwriting

> Most of us take for granted how easily we grip a pencil, write small letters, and keep them within the lines, but for some students, these seemingly simple processes tire them out.

output. For students who struggle to output their ideas, computers can be an incredible facilitator of their writing.

For our students with fine motor and/or visual processing challenges, handwriting requires an abundant amount of mental energy. Most of us take for granted how easily we grip a pencil, write small letters, and keep them within the lines, but for some students, these seemingly simple processes tire them out. Computer typing levels the playing field, taking these burdens off students' shoulders. With computer writing, you can also say goodbye to students' hand cramps and chicken-scratch sentences. But there are even more important reasons why digital writing can more effectively promote writing production.

Personally, I find typing extremely gratifying because I can produce letters and words rapidly. Even for slow typists, some simple tapping of keys produces thoughts and ideas instantly on the screen. Moving a pencil on a page feels different. Sluggish, I dare say. I'm sure some people disagree, people who cherish opportunities to sit with a journal and jot out memories or insights from their day. These people probably do not have writing production challenges.

And in my experience, it is far easier, more enjoyable, and more effective for students with attention challenges to produce their ideas using computers than it is to write by hand. For these kids, seeing their thoughts quickly appear on a screen in digital form can be far more gratifying than having to manipulate a pencil. Digital writing is all around them. It's what they're accustomed to reading. Documents on the computer look professional, like the writing they see on the internet, on TV, and in books. Seeing their ideas in Times New Roman—or even a tidy Arial or Calibri—gives them confidence, especially compared to their past messy attempts at handwriting, and may encourage further writing production.

It's also fun. After students have produced a sentence or a paragraph or an essay, they can manipulate the font, color, and size and make the text appear pleasing to their own eye; ultimately, they're taking ownership of it.

Another benefit of using the computer is that it also promotes editing. The standard writing process includes editing/revising of the rough draft, either with the teacher marking the mistakes or the student erasing errors and attempting to scrawl in the corrections. We ask students to do a final draft, so their writing will be presentable and free of mistakes. If students are writing by hand, they have to spend time and energy to write their paragraph or essay again, this time incorporating the corrections.

With digital writing, the burden of having to copy the writing is removed, and students can instead put their attention on editing right into the original document. Students can read their work and perform the editing changes while simultaneously creating an instantly clean, new draft. And doesn't this mimic the way adults edit their own work? We don't edit our emails, cover letters, and applications by creating a whole new draft; we make edits right in our original, rough documents, effectively cleaning them up until they appear like new drafts. To be clear, they're still doing a revision by finding errors and doing rewrites; the process is simply being streamlined.

Of course, pencil and paper are still a part of our lives. It's still valuable for a person to be able to pick up a pen and quickly jot down some ideas on a notepad. Maybe you need to fill out a job application on the spot or you're faced with important forms at the DMV or bank. Considering how pervasive technology is in young people's lives, school may be the only place where they get to practice writing with a pencil. For younger students who are just starting to develop early reading skills, studies have shown that handwriting helps with their visual recognition of letters. Given this, it's clearly important for kindergartners to practice writing letters and words with pencils.[8] And it is certainly valuable for teachers of any age group to include time for students to write out their ideas with good old-fashioned writing utensils and for students to learn how to write neatly enough for their words to be legible.

The key is that these handwriting opportunities—whether they're done with traditional pencils, mechanical pencils, or dry-erase markers—be small stakes. Don't make these end-of-unit projects or wall-fodder for open house. Pencils could be used at the brainstorming stage when students have to get down some simple ideas. Use handwriting for completing worksheets or jotting down the evening's homework.

Another issue that often arises is that some students type very slowly, and this is most often true of really young students. One solution is to get kids up and running on typing programs, many of which are free online. Dance Mat Typing, for example, is a lot of fun, with animated characters guiding the students through different levels. There are also games online in which the player must type quickly to blast planes out of the sky, shoot darts at balloons, or move a race car around a track. Fun and engaging!

GUEST SPEAKER
DON RICE

Don Rice is now a junior at a progressive private school. During his sophomore year, he not only wrote several short stories, but he also completed a full action/comedy novel over 25,000 words! Here he talks about his early struggles with writing and the factors that led him to improve his skills and develop a passion for creative writing.

Writing was always a challenge for me. When I was eight or nine, I would try to write simple paragraphs, and whether it was in class or in the comfort of my own home, it never went well. At the time, I just didn't want to do it. Generating ideas was really hard for me. I couldn't stand sitting in my chair and I just wanted to go watch TV. I understand now it had to do with my ADHD that I was later diagnosed with. My mom and dad would have to sit with me for hours to try to get me to finish assignments for school, and even just starting was nearly impossible; it was such a struggle. In fifth grade, I was asked to write typical essays, a few pages around 200 words, and it was a nightmare. I just couldn't jot down any of my thoughts on paper, even when I wanted to.

What's interesting is that, aside from writing, I was actually a very creative person with a lot of ideas. I remember waiting with my brother after school to be picked up, and to keep busy I would take the big colored paper from the art room and make cool monster cut outs that would fight each other with unique weapons. So really I was always a storyteller, I just couldn't write any of it down.

When I was in sixth grade, I started at a new school that was designed to help students like me. The school required students to have a laptop, so my parents provided me with one. Immediately, I felt more comfortable writing on my laptop than on paper. It was my personal portable device that I could use not only as entertainment but as my main source of writing tools: Microsoft Word and PowerPoint. Quickly, I realized that typing was so much easier for me than handwriting, and I could do so ten times as quickly.

Slowly, over the years, I completed a lot of creative writing exercises at school. As I started writing longer stories, I discovered my passion for creating new characters and plotlines. While improving my creative writing, I've also developed my overall writing skills for academic assignments. Now, when I have an essay to write for any subject, it's so much easier for me to get started.

Considering all those years I struggled with writing, it's amazing to think I might have never discovered my talent and interest in storytelling if I hadn't started writing on a computer.

What stands out to me in Don's story is that he always had creativity in him. He just couldn't express it using a pencil. When students have difficulty writing, it doesn't necessarily mean they have nothing to say; they just may not have found the writing mechanism that works for them. That Don has come so far as to complete an entire novel after struggling so greatly to write in elementary school is astonishing.

Another takeaway is that Don's interest and development as a creative writer led to his improvements in academic writing. Showing young students how enjoyable writing can be before teaching them expository writing can affect their overall attitude about composition in general.

Encourage Speech-to-Text

I've seen the future of typing, and it is called speech-to-text . . . or speech recognition . . . or voice typing. Whatever you call this tool, it's fantastic.

Personally, I use voice typing more and more every day, both with my phone and computer. Sometimes, it's just easier to get an idea across by speaking it, and voice recognition software is improving continually in its accuracy. I admit, when I first started using speech-to-text with students I was skeptical. I thought it would be too inaccurate, especially considering that our students often struggle with speech issues. Not only was this not an issue, but it actually helped students improve both their oral and written expressions.

ATTENTION GRABBER
Speaking of Success

I was a resource teacher in a second-grade classroom providing support to Anna and Jared, two students who were very outspoken with a lot to say but who wrote with extremely messy handwriting. Enormous letters broke above and below the lines like elephants trying to bust out of cages. Each student could barely produce a coherent sentence that was legible. Jared had never really shown interest in his own writing's content, and I believe it was due to the messy quality of the work. He would often tell me in a disappointed voice how messy his writing was.

I had access to two tablet computers on campus, so I opened up the Notes app and gave it a shot. Right away, the students were giddy to use the tablets. As they started to speak out their ideas, they witnessed their words popping up on the screen as if they were typing, receiving instant feedback on how their speaking sounded.

The story is about a girl with magic powers. She is the book's hero.

Anna had no speech difficulties, so she was fully up and running, producing more sentences than I'd ever seen from her. For Jared, speech was a significant issue. He tended to slur his words and speak very softly, making it difficult to understand him. Of course, seeing his words type out inaccurately was initially frustrating for him, but instead of nixing the tablet, I used it as an opportunity to encourage him to speak more clearly and more slowly. I modeled for him how to do so, articulating my words extra carefully. It wasn't difficult for him to emulate my speaking style and see how the accuracy improved. (This may not work for every student with speech challenges; for some students it may be too inaccurate and frustrating. See page 106 for another option for these students.)

Another huge benefit of speech-to-text is that it encourages students to take a few moments to consider exactly what they want to say. As Jared started to produce more writing on the tablet, he noticed that his sentences tended to be very short, just four to six words. Now that the aesthetics of his writing were clear and appealing, he could focus more on his actual ideas. With tablet in hand, he began to take a few seconds before speaking to consider what he wanted to say. With my encouragement, he added more detail to his thoughts and created more compelling sentences. Soon, he was writing longer sentences independently and increasing the amount of production as well.

When previously presented with writing tasks, Jared's head would often drop to the table as if he'd been told to run a marathon. Anna would often sit in her seat, unable to get started, a blank page staring at her for the duration of class. With speech-to-text, both students were more energized to speak their sentences and watch their ideas type out on the screen.

With Anna and Jared, I was able to spend the time to show them how to use the speech recognition function and to troubleshoot. If it's hard to find the time to do that during class, find another time to teach those specific students how to use the technology—during recess or lunch, or when there is some free time at the end of the day—so that later, when there is a writing assignment, they are prepared to jump in. (Older students probably understand how to use the technology better than we do.)

Kindergarten teachers often scribe for students who are not yet able to actually write out a sentence. How about having them try to scribe for themselves by using speech-to-text? It may be that much more engaging and gratifying for them to see their own spoken words type out on the screen, and like with Jared and Anna, it may prompt them to spend a few extra moments to consider how to phrase their sentence coherently before speaking. Again, at this young age, handwriting has many benefits, but including times for them to compose with technology may help spark more writing production.

Some have questioned me on this, asking if speech-to-text is really "writing." Writing is the act of putting thoughts and ideas in a form that can be read, using characters, words, symbols, and so on. Does it really matter how the ideas get from our brain to the paper? Whether we are handwriting, typing, or using speech-to-text, we are learning how to express ourselves through words that can be read by another person. Does the person reading know or care what

Whether we are handwriting, typing, or using speech-to-text, we are learning how to express ourselves through words that can be read by another person.

mechanism the author used? I feel confident in saying, and I think most would agree, that Stephen Hawking is the author of his ground-breaking book, *A Brief History of Time*, even though he could not physically write the book and used some form of alternative writing system.

Here are some other benefits of this interface.

To include punctuation in the writing, you actually speak the words "comma," "period," "question mark," and so on. This is an effective reinforcement for students to be attentive to punctuation in general and to choose the appropriate mark at the right point in the sentence. For example, it's a fantastic opportunity to teach students to take a breath after they complete a thought, and to either put a comma or period. From there, you can teach further about compound sentences.

How easily accessible are speech-to-text apps?

Most phones and tablets now have the capability either built into their virtual keyboards or as an option in their settings. Most devices also have some sort of notes app that can serve as a virtual piece of paper. A student can speak into the app and create a note that they can submit to you via email, the cloud, or a website. Or they can send it to themselves to convert to a word processing or slides document—or print it out—before turning it in.

All new Mac computers have this function built in. No matter what program, app, or online site you're using, you can simply double tap the "fn" button and the speech-to-text function appears automatically. Google Drive has also made this feature readily accessible regardless of the platform. A speech-to-text function is available in both Google Docs and Slides in their online cloud drive of apps. In Docs, you can verbally input writing directly into the main document space. In Slides, this function forces you to input the writing into the "Speak Notes" section at the bottom of the page. There are also independent apps you can download onto your computer or tablet. The most well-known of these is Dragon Dictation.

Sometimes voice-to-text does not work for a student. I once had a student who acted too silly when using it, oftentimes speaking song lyrics that were totally off topic or saying inappropriate things to watch the words type out on the screen. Unfortunately, he couldn't control his impulses, so I could not use this function with him. And for some students, speech issues may interfere with the accuracy of voice recognition.

If for whatever reason voice-to-text is not a viable option for certain students, you can have those students dictate their ideas to you, and you do the typing. Again, this does not mean you're doing the writing for them. You are simply acting as the tool by which the thoughts and ideas get down into readable form. It also gives you the opportunity to quickly reteach or reinforce writing skills, including grammar rules, organization, and clarity. You could ask students to speak out the punctuation to you, like they would using a voice recognition app, or you could just type out exactly what they say without punctuation and have them go through the text afterward to add periods and commas and fix the grammar. Another option is to assign students to work in pairs, matching strong typists with students who can use the help.

Allow Slide-Making Programs

Back in grad school, I had to make a slideshow for a class, and I fell in love . . . with slide-making programs.

No, this is not the plot to the movie *Her*.

With apps like PowerPoint and Google Slides, you can easily add pictures and move them around and create text boxes and put them wherever you want. You can change colors of text and add outlines to images. Ultimately, these programs offer a lot of freedom to how you design your pages. But best of all, once you have the basics down, these interfaces are super easy to navigate.

Both word processors and slide programs are tools that serve the same purpose: The users get their ideas, thoughts, and information into written form to teach an audience something. In my experience, slide programs result in more sustained attention and production from students with attention deficits, which is why I usually teach my students to use PowerPoint instead of Word, or Google Slides instead of Docs.

Another big factor is that slide programs are a more engaging way to teach organization. Whether a student is at the paragraph or essay stage of writing, these programs can help teach students how to separate their ideas and information and put them in proper sequence. Teaching students to create separate slides for subtopics helps them learn how to structure their written work. For example, if a student is learning how to build a paragraph, the first slide could say "Topic Sentence" at the top, the next three slides could be "Detail 1," "Detail 2," and "Detail 3," and the final slide could say "Closing Sentence." For essays, the first slide could be "Introduction," with the three body paragraphs as the next three slides, and then "Conclusion" for the final slide.

Theoretically, you could use Word or Google Docs to do all of the suggestions above. Here's the difference. Each slide functions like a canvas, free of limitations. Users can create text boxes with a click of the button and type in information and ideas, pick a font and size, and then move this

TOPIC SENTENCE

Camping can be a fun experience.

text box wherever they want. Word processors function in invisible lines; it can be frustrating to move text or pictures around the page and to try to place them exactly how you want them, especially when there are also words on the page—it's very cumbersome because the programs weren't designed to do that.

With slide programs, it is incredibly easy to search the web for an appropriate picture, drag it onto the canvas, and then reshape it or move it wherever the student wants it to go. In other words, it allows for more creativity in how the student wants to present the information. I often have students first find pictures for their information and place them on the slides; this helps them feel like they've made a dent in their assignment, removing more of the anxiety-provoking blankness from the slides. It also gives them some visuals that provide inspiration for their ideas.

ATTENTION GRABBER
Big Cat Slide Show

In my after-school sessions with Lee, a fifth-grade student, I tried to lower his anxiety with fun, short writing tasks that allowed him to produce in low pressure situations. I could see he possessed writing skills and ideas, but his anxiety, along with his production difficulty, prevented him from producing much of anything, especially writing. His teacher had assigned a long-term research essay project on extinct animals. Lee was very excited to learn more about prehistoric cheetahs, but I was concerned about his ability to handle a five-paragraph essay. I suggested to the teacher, and she was amenable, that we give him the option of using PowerPoint slides to present his research instead of a typical essay on Word.

Immediately, he was engaged with creating an outline of his project by adding five slides to the presentation to represent the essay's five paragraphs. At school, he was able to generate questions about extinct cheetahs, which he narrowed down to three subtopics. I guided him to label the three middle slides, each with one of the subtopics: physical characteristics, survival, and evolution.

Once Lee had the five slides organized, including introduction and conclusion slides, he could start considering which of his researched information to put on each page. At school, the teacher encouraged him to use different color fonts to distinguish between the subtopics. Brilliant. This further helped him internalize how to organize information into smaller compartments. And giving him creative license to pick the colors, select pictures, and design each slide engaged him more than I'd ever seen him while writing. Normally, he'd show little pride in his work, but this time he was very excited to actually print out his slide show, hold the final product in his hands, and put it in his backpack to bring back to school.

Ultimately, the student's original writing for each slide remained brief, but for him, that was okay. The organizational skills he learned from this process was a great foundation for his five-paragraph essay writing in the future.

If you're having students use computers for writing in class, make slide programs available along with word processors. You could even do a lesson about the major functions. Of course, given that students have grown up with technology, they probably already know how to use them or at least could pick it up very quickly.

The Big Takeaway

Knowing how to type and use computer programs and online apps are crucial skills in the 21st century. While it's fine to continue to have students write with pen and pencil sometimes, and some of them may even prefer this, our students with attention deficits often struggle with this mode of writing. For them, typing, voice-to-text, and slide programs can be extremely beneficial tools to use on their journey as writers. These options can remove the obstacles of graphomotor and visual integration challenges, give more creative freedom, increase writing fluency, reduce anxiety, and raise confidence.

> Imagine trying to cut your lawn with a handsaw or eat spaghetti with a spoon. We want to prevent this sort of frustration by finding the right writing mechanism for struggling students.

Imagine trying to cut your lawn with a handsaw or eat spaghetti with a spoon. We want to prevent this sort of frustration and low work production by finding the right writing mechanism for struggling students. And it's not going to be the same for everybody. Try different things. Experiment.

We can also set up reachable goals for our students by shortening assignments or breaking down larger ones, so students can feel accomplished by completing smaller steps, like filling out a bubble map, creating an outline, or just writing the introduction as a preliminary goal. Put students in a position to experience writing victories and gain confidence so they're willing to engage with progressively more challenging tasks.

When you put these struggling writers in a position to express their ideas like their peers can, their sense of empowerment is thrilling to see.

CHAPTER 5

MAKE A LONG STORY *FEEL* SHORT
How to Engage Students in the Reading Process

I don't enjoy going to Shakespeare plays. There, I said it.

Before you judge, let me explain.

The play starts, and I can hang with it for a few minutes. My input abilities work overtime to help process the unusual language and figure out the names and details of each new character and their relationships to one another. But then the dialogue starts coming fast and furious. Someone seems upset . . . but why? This character clearly is in love with another character . . . but which? This guy seems to be plotting something dastardly . . . but what? This is about the point when my mind starts to tune out and wander to who-knows-where. Suddenly, I come to attention, and it's now Act II, and someone has taken over the throne, and I have no idea what the heck is going on. Have I mentioned that I was an English literature major in college?

Trust me, I want to stay alert when I see Shakespeare. But the combination of comprehending oral language and keeping my input abilities working makes it very challenging for me.

I imagine this is how some students feel in classrooms every day, just trying to absorb and comprehend all of the language thrown at them. And they can feel this even more strongly when assigned to read challenging text such as novels, especially long ones. With some students, it is difficult to say where a language processing issue stops and an attention issue starts. And sometimes, it's a confluence of the two.

Most of my students with attention challenges are resistant to reading for fun. It takes so much mental energy for them to process so much language at once, they ultimately get turned off. Being able to read for extended periods is a valuable skill, necessary to read a lengthy contract, an informative magazine article, Yelp reviews to help you spend your dollars wisely, or a nonfiction book that could help you through a difficult time. On top of that, reading is enriching.

Students with challenges need support accessing books and literature, both fiction and nonfiction; they deserve the chance to become readers for life.

This chapter does not offer strategies to develop students' cognitive processes of reading and language comprehension. For that, there are plenty of books and resources to help you target specific skills and domains, and if you have students with phonics, fluency, or comprehension challenges, those must be recognized and attended to either in your classroom or with outside support. A student's receptive language issues will most certainly affect their engagement with texts, whatever they may be.

What you'll find here are tools to help you engage students with your chosen material, regardless of how challenging the reading itself may be. These are strategies that cover both the reading and pre-reading phases, and while many of the strategies relate specifically to literature, most can also be applied to any sort of fiction or nonfiction text, short or long; this topic is certainly relevant to social sciences, history, or any subject that may use a textbook or written resources.

Frontload Key Story Elements and Information

Many teachers prepare their students for novels with several strategies. They'll give students background information—maybe watch a video about the author, look at some pictures or artwork from the time period, or learn about related historical events—to help students place the story in context. They may also have students make predictions about characters and plot. All of these strategies help prime students' comprehension and interest in the material.

For students with attention challenges who struggle with complicated texts, these supports may not be enough. Analyzing literature, history, and other such material requires a lot of background knowledge, higher-order thinking skills, and even life experience. Throw in an attention-related input challenge, and a student can really struggle.

To help engage students with the material early, try *frontloading*. If you're about to assign a text with difficult language, have the students read a short summary of the plot before starting. They could also read character breakdowns and some short analyses of the major themes. These sorts of summaries are readily available online. For many books, you can even find short videos that preview the major characters and plot points; many of them are animated and pretty entertaining. Shmoop.com produces summary videos with an acerbic wit, and author John Green usually starts his incredibly entertaining and sharp analysis videos (on the YouTube channel Crash Course) with short animations that give you the main plot points and characters. You don't necessarily have to do this for the whole class. You could just take a bit of extra time to help frontload some story information with your students who could most benefit from it.

To some, this may sound crazy. One might argue that the whole point of reading is to experience the story as it happens, to slowly process the events and effectively change your thinking as you continue to read. But if a student doesn't have the input abilities to sustain prolonged processing of language, none of that will happen anyway. CliffsNotes are only a bad thing if a student is using it secretly as a means for *not* reading the book. Frontloading has a whole different purpose. I have used this approach numerous times, and I've observed that knowing the basic plot, characters, and themes ahead of time helps students feel more at ease with the material.

This strategy can also be applied to reading assignments in textbooks, whether it's social science, history, or economics. For example, if you've assigned a chapter for homework about the Scientific

Revolution, you can preview subtopics like the geocentric theory, the heliocentric theory, and the scientific method before you send students home that night. You could show some related images, such as the solar system and early telescopes. In another approach to the same chapter, you could give students some quick information about the dominant figures like Galileo, Newton, Kepler, and Copernicus and offer some artists' depictions of them. Then when they go home and read the chapter, they will already have a base understanding of the themes and ideas. This doesn't have to be significant; try a quick five- to ten-minute preview.

In this age of "spoilers," people are rabid about avoiding them because they don't want to know what happens in their favorite TV show. The mystery of not knowing what's going to happen makes people want to keep watching. So isn't telling students too much about the book up front like giving students spoilers? Won't it make them less likely to want to read a book if they already know some of the plot points?

That's not what I've found. In fact, I've seen the opposite happen.

ATTENTION GRABBER
Greasers to the Rescue

Xavier, a sixth grader, was about to read *The Outsiders* with his class. Despite the gripping story and memorable lines like "Stay gold, Ponyboy," I knew sustaining engagement would be tough. Xavier loved stories, whether in graphic novels, comics, or video games—he would talk endlessly about the video game franchise *Five Nights at Freddy's*—but he had significant attention issues and anxiety with reading, especially when he was confronted with an abundant amount of language.

When his teacher told me he'd be reading *The Outsiders*, I knew immediately there was an easy way in for Xavier: the 1983 movie. He isn't a huge movie fan, which is surprising because he clearly loves images; aside from comics and video games, he always wanted to show me the latest memes he was into (perhaps movies offer too much information and move too quickly for him to process at once). I searched for images online of the film, and there were shots of Patrick Swayze, Rob Lowe, C. Thomas Howell, Ralph Macchio, Matt Dillon, and Tom Cruise as the main characters. I quickly threw them onto a slideshow and labeled them with their corresponding character names. I also included other images from the web that showed scenes of action.

Xavier was totally engrossed by the images. He kept laughing, asking me about the slick hairstyles and strange clothing the guys wore. We talked about greasers and how that was the style of "bad boys" back in the 50s and 60s—also checking out Fonzie and the Beatles as teenagers.

Knowing the book contained a lot of slang from the era that would only add to his language comprehension demands, I also put some words on a slide, including the "fuzz" (cops), a "heater" (gun), a "hood" (criminal), and "tuff/rank" (cool, uncool).

Some of the images showed youngsters fighting and holding knives, including guys who looked a lot different from the greasers, dressed in nice, fancy clothes. I told him these were the "Socs" (pronouncing it "soashes"), the rival group of boys who hated the greasers. This piqued his interest, and he was curious to know some of the plot details. I told him that there would be scenes of huge fights between them, and some characters would get really hurt.

And that some characters would even die.

He begged me to tell him which characters, but I told him "No spoilers."

Actually, I *was* giving him spoilers, enough to give him a general idea of the plot, characters, and setting, but not enough to make him feel like he'd already read the story.

As he proceeded to read with the class and by himself at home, he kept trying to get me to tell him who would die. I just kept dangling it in front of him, saying "You'll see if you keep reading!"

With my students who struggle to read entire novels, giving them spoilers, just small ones, of course, appears to increase their engagement and desire to read further. The reason, in my opinion, is because now they have some groundwork for their own comprehension. And now they want to read how the characters get to those spoiler moments. In other words, it piques their interest instead of deflating it.

It doesn't have to take a lot of extra prep time to put these previews together. Find some relevant images online, drag them onto slides, and add some text regarding the basic elements you think should be previewed. No need for it to look fancy. It just needs to transmit the information clearly. In fact, you may not have to do any prep at all; you can find many slide shows already made by teachers online. If you want to preview a specific book or topic, just do a search on the web, or try teacherspayteachers.com.

If this still sounds like I'm endorsing cheating, think of it this way: Frontloading some of the story and narrative elements is like having students watch a highly detailed movie trailer before seeing a movie.

I love movie trailers. The good ones can get us excited about seeing a movie we hadn't yet heard about. As a secondary effect, they show us the main characters, some pertinent information about them, and their primary struggles. They even give us some specific story events, different settings, and exciting moments that are clearly turning points. When you go into a movie already knowing some key story elements, it allows you to feel secure in your understanding of what's happening. And because your brain doesn't have to work as hard at the outset to establish who, what, and where, you can focus more on details.

> Frontloading some of the story and narrative elements is like having students watch a highly detailed movie trailer before seeing a movie.

If you don't want to give a detailed preview to the whole class, just make time to give the students who need it a preview of the book so they have a base understanding of what's to come. This way, they feel more confident in their basic knowledge of the story elements and can put more of their mental energy on comprehending the language.

Use Audiobooks

"My child just won't read for fun."

I can't tell you how many times I've heard that from parents. Reading books can be incredibly difficult and stressful for students with attention challenges. Of course, there may be a concurrent language processing issue and/or dyslexia, but even when students' fluency levels are at grade level, they may be reticent to read for sustained periods of time. By the time students come home from school, they have endured a full day of burdens on their attention functions. And now they have to summon more mental energy, focus their eyes and brains, and concentrate on making sense of a bunch of paragraphs of words. They're tired. They just want to watch some TV, play a few video games, and hit the hay. But they've got three chapters of *The Book Thief* to read for tomorrow.

What if the story is read to them? Behold, the wonder of audiobooks.

Audiobooks can be a powerful tool for reluctant readers to use at home or at school when given time to read independently. For students with attention and language challenges, using headphones can help keep them on task, and being able to control the volume of the narration can be effective in engaging them with the narrator. To improve fluency and comprehension, students can sometimes adjust the pace at which the narrator reads.[9]

There are potential downsides with this scenario. Many teachers argue that listening to an audiobook is not really reading because it takes the decoding aspect out of the equation. Another issue is that in our lives, we are called upon constantly to read on the spot, both on the computer and out in the world, so learning to process written information for sustained periods is a very important skill for students to develop. These are totally valid concerns.

Here are some things to consider. The first is that if decoding or fluency is a problem area for students, they will be better served practicing these skills in isolation with shorter texts at the appropriate Lexile level. If the assigned book is beyond the student's Lexile level, it may not be beneficial to force the student to spend so much energy decoding or trying to read it fluently. Their comprehension may suffer, and thus they'll lose engagement with the text. In other words, this assigned book may not be the time to focus on the visual component of reading but rather on comprehension, which can happen though auditory means.

Professor Gene Wolfson argues in his 2008 article, "Using Audiobooks to Meet the Needs of Adolescent Readers," that the literacy skills and strategies students use while listening to a story read to them are the same as if they were reading themselves. But by removing the burden of visual decoding and word recognition, students can focus more attention on meaning. The audiobook may be just the support students need to continue developing the literacy and comprehension skills Wolfson is referring to—and, not to mention, feel like part of the class.

Second, I strongly suggest to my students that they follow along with the text as they listen to the audiobook. This is especially important for students with auditory comprehension deficits. For them, it is very challenging to process information when it's only given through sound. Students should hold the actual book and attempt to follow the words on the pages while they hear the story. This is similar to how teachers read aloud in class while students follow along in their own copies.

Audiobooks are read by actors who bring the story to life by infusing emotion into the narration and characters. More crucially, it takes the burden off students having to process the language alone. As they follow along with the text in the book, they are still reading, but it's almost as if the audiobook adds training wheels to their sustained attention. They're still peddling and steering, but if their attention wavers a bit, they won't fall on their face.

And the training wheels will come off. I've seen how using audiobooks can lead to students eventually reading independently without them.

ATTENTION GRABBER
Audio of the Flies

Several times I've had students who were assigned *Lord of the Flies*, which contains an inordinate amount of description in the form of long, poetic paragraphs depicting the jungle and everything in it.

One of these students was Sierra, an eighth grader who was struggling to read novels independently due to her attention and language processing challenges. I listened to her read the opening pages of the book, and at the end of some of the long paragraphs, she'd say, "Wait, what happened?" This sort of struggle to understand the content would wear her out, and she wouldn't want to engage with the book for longer than a few minutes. The chapters in *Lord of the Flies* happen to be quite long as well, which didn't help her confidence in proceeding forward; she would constantly count the pages remaining until the next chapter and be dismayed at how far away that goal appeared. Overall, it was incredibly difficult for her to sustain attention on reading and understand these paragraphs.

I soon tracked down a copy of the audiobook at a nearby library and brought it to Sierra to see if this would benefit her. (Not every attention grabber works for every student.) I could see the difference immediately. The author himself, William Golding, was reading the text, with his bass-filled voice and British accent. An actor or great orator can really bring a book to life. I could almost see Sierra's ears shoot up, now attuned to the soothing narration.

But here's what really surprised me. Sierra didn't just rely on the audio. Instead, she instinctively followed along in the book, moving her finger along the words as Golding read them.

Another cool feature of audiobooks is that they give students a fun sort of control over the material. If Sierra did lose focus for a few seconds or lose comprehension, she would immediately skip back the audio to hear it again. She was drawn into the narrative quickly, so she was motivated to understand every new piece of information about Jack, Ralph, Piggy, and the rest.

Sierra got a copy of the audiobook for home so she could read on her own, in class, and also with me during our sessions. She continued to be engaged with the novel for the duration, always eager to give me her thoughts on the exciting plot turns!

Later in the year, I noticed her start to read and comprehend more text on her own. She was no longer asking me to explain the content. When it came to the final book of the school year, *Animal Farm*, she no longer needed the training wheels.

Perhaps you could take time to play pieces of the audiobook for the whole class, especially the parts that have particularly difficult language or complicated plot events. Audible, Amazon's subscription-based service of audiobooks, has just about every title you'd look for in audio format. If you have a computer in class, you could download the book or get the CDs from the library or online and create a listening station for any student who could benefit from it. You could also encourage particular students and their parents to get hold of the audiobook for home.

Use Ebooks

Truth be told, I like to hold a book in my hands when I read. I enjoy admiring the cover artwork and reading the back matter and blurbs. For most of us, the small letter size in books doesn't bother us, and we're okay with the lack of spacing between lines of text. But for our students with attention challenges, these visual constraints might make it difficult for them to read for sustained periods, forcing them to use too much mental energy just to process the abundant amount of letters, words, and paragraphs stuffed onto a single page. I often teach students how to hold bookmarks sideways on the page to cover up the lines above where they're reading, moving it down line by line as they continue on.

Of course, as we get older, we acquire reading glasses to help alleviate the strain on our eyes, but for our students, ebooks are a much more effective alternative support that can be downloaded onto tablets, laptops, or desktop computers. E-readers have the potential to support struggling readers due to the many tools and features that allow the reader to physically interact with and manipulate the text, making the reading experience interactive and engaging. These include a digital interface that allows students to zoom in and magnify the words or change the font size to their preference. They can often use a dictionary feature, which lets them click on a word they don't know and learn its meaning. And they

> E-readers can support struggling readers with features that allow the reader to physically interact with and manipulate the text, making the reading experience interactive and engaging.

even have a text-to-speech feature that will pronounce difficult words for them. With these features, digital readers can function like a support teacher or tutor. Overall, studies have shown comprehension improvements with students using e-readers. As the ebook features help students with comprehension, students' engagement with the text should increase.

True, the risk is there that the features and interface could add to their distraction. And if they're reading on a tablet or a computer, they can very easily get off task by searching the web or opening a game app. For middle schoolers, the temptations of social media are also ever present. This is an opportunity for our students to practice impulse control. Being able to work on a computer without becoming distracted frequently is important considering how many of our tasks, whether at work or in our lives, are done online. Speaking with students about this challenge can be a start to their self-management of online activity. For each student, identify the specific distraction that gives them trouble—games, messaging, sports scores, and such—and discuss the appropriate times that student could engage with these things. We can teach students how to set timers for themselves, which is easy to do on electronic devices, and give themselves breaks after they apply the appropriate amount of time to tasks (timers are covered further in chapter 7).

The reality may be that a student isn't ready to refrain from impulses to check social media and surf the web, so an ebook may not work. As I often say, it's worth a shot.

There are also websites like newsela.com and myon.com that teachers can sign up for, giving their students access to digital reading content. Newsela mainly contains articles keeping up with current events, and you can pick from three or four different Lexile levels for each article. There are also comprehension questions and writing prompts. MyON has news articles and a ton of fiction stories as well, including the full texts of classic novels, shorter books for younger students, and short nonfiction books covering a variety of topics. It offers a lot of interactive tools students can use while reading, including highlighters and digital sticky notes. It also tailors recommendations to the students' interests and reading levels.

I have slowly been adding e-reading to my diet, and I must say, it can be fun even for a traditionalist like me. Personally, I love being able to zoom in or make the font bigger so my eyes don't strain. I love being able to define any word I don't understand or, if there's a reference to something I'm not aware of, quickly looking it up online. And I admit, flipping the "pages" by swiping is pretty cool.

Find Graphic Novel Versions

Looking at a graphic novel is like reading a movie. The great ones offer an experience just as rewarding as reading a great novel or watching a riveting film. And every year, more graphic novel versions of classics are being published. I have found versions for my own students that include *Romeo and Juliet, Macbeth, Frankenstein, The Odyssey*, and *Fahrenheit 451*. Graphic novels are similar to summaries in giving students a base understanding of the main characters, story events, and ideas of the novels. They also help crystallize the characters and details to give students a more tangible picture to keep in mind as they read the original novel.

In addition to fiction, you can also find graphic novels depicting historical events, biographies of important figures—even scientific concepts. These versions bring the stories to life in a way that textbooks, while offering much more information, just cannot do. It makes them feel more like typical stories being told, and this in itself can be engaging for students.

Again, these are not a replacement for other material. Students should read these either before they attempt the source material or read it concurrently.

ATTENTION GRABBER
Percy Jackson—A Life in Pictures

My seventh-grade student, Mikayla, had come a long way. Her phonics decoding and fluency had greatly improved since she was in fifth grade, when I started working with her. She had increased her words per minute by about thirty words in those two years, and now she was able to sustain engagement with entire novels. She loved books about middle school drama (the sort that happens between friends), but she was still a bit resistant to other genres. She'd made it through *Hatchet* earlier in the year, but that's a short book. In the latter half of the year, she'd been assigned *Percy Jackson and the Olympians*.

This was a big deal for her. First, she'd never read a fantasy novel like this with so much action happening in every chapter and so many characters to keep track of. On top of that, this book has lots of information about actual mythology. Usually students learn about Greek mythology as a whole independent unit, but in this book, the reader must not only digest the plot and characters but simultaneously learn new information about all sorts of gods, their powers, and their relationships to each other. With so much information to input and comprehend, a book like this can feel overwhelming to an emerging reader.

Second, this would be the longest book she'd attempted to read, by far. To be honest, it was hard for me to imagine her getting through it. Her comprehension was pretty good—she didn't often need explanation of what she'd read—but she tended to fatigue after reading a few pages, and often, when I asked her to recall details about the story, it was difficult for her to remember a lot.

She read the first couple of chapters, and she was definitely into the story, but when she told me how much she'd have to read for the next day, she sounded overwhelmed.

That's when I went to the library and checked out the graphic novel of *Percy Jackson*. During our next session, she started looking at the pictures and reading the text and dialogue bubbles. Soon she began to notice that the graphic novel was leaving out a lot of events from the book. It actually sparked her memory about scenes she'd read, which formerly was difficult for her. She then flipped through the graphic novel some more and found the exact ways that it was shortening the actual novel.

During subsequent sessions, as she made her way through the novel on her own, slowly but surely, she checked in with the graphic novel, found the section that corresponded to the chapters she'd read during the week, and listed the pieces of the story it was leaving out. She was using it as a reference book, of sorts, a graphic outline to help her recognize the major plot points and characterizations.

It also prompted her to think critically. She kept wondering why certain parts had been left out of the graphic novel, which led to some great discussions about what plot points were really crucial to the main story and which could be snipped out.

As she neared the end of the book, she was given an assignment by her classroom teacher to choose a memorable scene and make an art project depicting the characters and action. It would have been easy for her to simply peruse the graphic novel and pick one that was already represented in pictures for her, but she picked one of the scenes the graphic novel omitted! This told me that she wasn't just relying on the graphic novel for comprehension. The graphic novel had helped engage her to the actual book and give her some images to spark her imagination, but she had grown confident enough in her understanding of the dense text that she chose a scene she'd only read about in the actual novel.

Having students read the original book and graphic novel concurrently encourages them to figure out what the graphic novel includes of the actual text and what it leaves on the cutting-room floor. When I do this with students, they often say things like, "Why didn't they include that scene from the book in the graphic novel?"

It's a great question to pose formally to your students. Ask them why they think the graphic novel writers and artists chose to keep certain scenes but omit others. This could serve as a writing prompt or something students could try to answer as they read. It's a great jumping off point to discuss plot, character, and even themes— perhaps they only kept in scenes and side plots truly relevant to the main themes of the book.

Something else I often hear is, "This isn't how I would draw that character." I love hearing these comments because it shows students are engaged with the material enough to have a strong opinion about it. For younger students, you could have them look at the comic pictures and then draw the way they see the characters. This, too, could act as a writing assignment, either a quick-write or longer project, in which students explain why they drew the characters as they did and discuss how the choices they made are different from the illustrator of the graphic novel. The next time you're choosing a new novel to teach, do some searches online to see which books have graphic novel versions available—and consider having students read both.

Teach How to Make Text Connections

When I consider the movies or books I love, I realize that my affinity for them is most often associated with personal connections. When we identify with characters, relate to things that happen in stories and in history, or consider our own feelings about ideas or concepts, we are instantly more engaged. Most of us probably do this instinctively, not only when we are absorbing stories or information, but in social situations as well. We often make connections in conversations between the other person and our own experiences or thoughts.

Students with input challenges may not know how to make connections, and so we have to teach about connections explicitly. I've seen many classroom teachers use text connections as a means of supporting comprehension and increasing engagement. It's a tool that works. This strategy can be especially effective for students with attention deficits, especially when it's applied regularly and methodically.

Though there are variations of this methodology, one effective approach is to highlight three types of connections: text-to-self, text-to-text, and text-to-world.

Text-to-self means a connection between the story, characters, or information and one's own experiences. If I'm reading *The Catcher in the Rye*, I might connect Holden's favorite red hunting hat to my own Red Sox hat that I wore in my youth. It gave me such comfort, even if I was stressed or sad about something . . . I wonder if Holden's hat gave him comfort? When students of mine are about to start reading a novel, I first try to figure out if there may be some sort of personal connection they may have to it. For example, before reading *From the Mixed-Up Files of Mrs. Basil E. Frankweiler*, I spoke with one of my students about my own dreams when I was a child of hiding out and sleeping over in the Boston Museum of Science where my class went on field trips. Then I asked him if there was any building, store, or place where he wished he could hide out for a while on his own. His answer? Dave & Buster's arcade and restaurant, of course! When students can identify with characters or situations in a book, it makes the story more relevant to them, making the author's themes and ideas inherently more engaging.

Text-to-text means a connection to another story, movie, TV show, or text of any kind. I could connect the book *City of Ember* with *The Giver* because they both have small communities whose residents think they are the only villages in existence as well as lead characters who want to discover if there is more out there. When prompting your students to make text-to-text connections to what you're reading, this is a great time to call attention to students' favorite movies, TV shows, and books (remember the interest survey from page 17). Can you prompt your students to make connections from the book you're reading in class to their favorites?

Some of our biggest pop culture entertainment, like the Star Wars and Marvel superhero universes, are so vast and include so many stories and different types of characters that there are myriad ways for students to make connections to them. You could ask students outright: "Can anyone think of a connection between the struggle for power in *Macbeth* to anything in Star Wars or Marvel?" Maybe one student suggests the battles for the throne in *Black Panther*. Another student may bring up the internal conflict of Anakin Skywalker and how he, like Macbeth, succumbs to the dark side. Could any of these connections lead to a writing project?

Text-to-world means a connection to anything out there beyond oneself or other texts. It may be something a student saw on YouTube or something that's been in the news. I once had a student who was reading a text about the religious intolerance prevalent in some of the original New England colonies, and he connected this to the intolerance toward African Americans that Martin Luther King Jr. fought against.

When students make connections to texts, it gives them a personal entry point to help them comprehend the material and concepts. It makes it relevant to them. It makes it accessible. Once they connect to information, they want to learn more and see if there are other ways it might be personally relevant to them. Students may also be more likely to remember the information and details because they have an idea they've brought to the table that is now a part of the text.

ATTENTION GRABBER
A Revolutionary Connection

Joshua, one of my fourth-grade students on the autism spectrum, had difficulty sustaining mental energy on reading for long periods of time, and his class was about to read *Ben and Me*, a historical fiction novel about a mouse who befriends Ben Franklin. I'd noticed in our after-school sessions that Joshua was an excellent decoder, and his fluency was about at grade level, but it was still a strain for him to input all the character and plot information. When I asked him for details about things he'd read independently, usually key details were missing. It appeared that he was rushing through the reading to get it over with, since the process fatigued him. This maybe explained why he was not reading much for fun.

I'd already taught him how to make connections while reading, working on the skills in isolation with short passages. It had sparked a lot of conversation between us—about things he'd experienced, things he knew about the world, or information he'd learned in class. I was starting to see how enthusiastic he could be in conversations when something sparked his memory and interest. *Ben and Me* would be the perfect opportunity to use those same connections skills to help him engage with a whole novel.

In preparation for reading the book, Joshua's teacher had already done a lot of prep with the class about Ben Franklin and his maxims as well as the colonial period. Joshua was still not excited to start reading the book, and he made this clear both in his words and his facial expressions.

I knew he enjoyed typing, so I created a slide show with a graphic organizer containing boxes for each chapter, and in the middle of the page I typed in "Joshua's Connections." While he read each chapter, I prompted him to find some sort of connection to the story or characters. In chapter one, he made the connection to *Stuart Little*, another story about a talking mouse. In chapter three, "The Bargain," he made a connection to the bargain he once made with his parents in which he would finish his history homework before going to his favorite entertainment center to play laser tag and video games. In chapter five, he connected the printing press to his family's digital printer at home. By this time, I no longer had to ask him to make connections; he was instinctively looking for ways to relate to Ben, the mouse, and their adventures.

By chapters eight and nine, Joshua was no longer showing any hesitation toward reading the book, and so I faded out use of the slide show. He was picking up more details about the characters and story, even while reading independently, and he was actually looking forward to finding out what happened next.

As I did with Joshua, you could have all your students keep a "Connections Log" and jot down any connections they make to the characters or story.

Making connections can also be reinforced during casual conversations, helping students with attention challenges and social issues relate to their peers. Consider how often in our everyday conversations we make connections to what the other person says. You could even make this into an informal game with students, where one person starts with something they did over the weekend, and the next person has to say something that is connected to that—something about herself or the world. This could be a fun warm-up game at the start of class or a quick refresher when students come back from recess.

GUEST SPEAKER
CHRIS WIEBE, Ed.D.

Chris Wiebe is now the principal of a private high school, but previously he was a humanities teacher in secondary classrooms. He has a real passion for literature, and here he talks about how he used a student's personal interest and expertise as a gateway into a literary classic.

Selling the importance of classic literature to the 21st-century student is tricky business. For students who grew up in the digital age with quick access to a seemingly limitless amount of information, trudging through *The Great Gatsby* can be even less appealing than it was for pre-internet students. Bringing students with attention issues into this playing field often requires individualized scaffolding.

For instance, Marcus, a student with high-anxiety and ADHD, was having trouble connecting with the novel. As the class confronted prompts about the complexities of Gatsby's past, or the symbolism of the green light at the end of the pier, Marcus was making no progress on reading assignments and becoming overwhelmed during class discussions, often acting out due to his frustrations—calling out, walking out of class, and so on.

As we made our way through the book, I noticed a few rare moments when Marcus did participate verbally, but these were only with regard to a specific interest. He fixated on questions about the book's geography: "How far is East Egg from West Egg?" "How many square miles is the Valley of Ashes?" I had known he was into science topics, but his unique interest in maps was a revelation. I realized I had my entry point.

I appointed Marcus class cartographer. He proactively printed out maps of the Long Island Sound—upon which the geographics of *Gatsby* are loosely based—then went to work with colored pencils, annotating maps with aerial and topographical views with the key points of interest in the text. Each class period, he would have time to share his work and discoveries with the class. Before the map project, he was not able to write a word about the novel or what we were discussing. As he became more comfortable with the text, his more scientific physical descriptions gave way to more conceptual reflections. Once he could visualize the location of the light at the end of the dock, which was sort of a middle ground between East and West Egg, he began to grapple with the thematic dichotomies between Gatsby's past and his ambitions for the future.

At the end of the book, Marcus delivered a poignant monologue about the catastrophic implications of class disparities, as evoked during the fateful car crash that destroys several characters' lives. It was incredible how far he came from not engaging with the book at all to this sort of critical analysis. It all started with his interest in the story's geography.

It's so inspiring to hear that a student who couldn't engage with a novel was able to do so through a specific talent. And it was impressive that Chris recognized that talent and effectively gave the student the time and encouragement to pursue that specific entry point. Though *Gatsby* does lend itself well to a geographical study, I think Marcus's interest could probably be applied to most books or topics. Certainly, in any history unit it would be easy to engage him in his map skills, and every novel takes place in some physical location that could be explored further.

Of course, it may be difficult if the student's interest or talent does not generally lend itself to texts—dancing, for instance. But let's consider how you could use that: How about asking the student to design a dance that matches a scene in the book or find a dance video online that may connect to the character? It may take some deep consideration on your part, but with a student who just can't connect to the material, it's worth brainstorming to see if you can find that entry point.

The Big Takeaway

Students with attention challenges often struggle with reading comprehension. While this may be due to a language-processing issue or other deficit, it may also be that their input abilities are not strong enough to sustain the processing of information for extended periods, which makes it very challenging for them to read and understand books or longer texts. The sad result is that the students hate reading.

We have to help change that.

Giving students summaries of characters, events, and themes as a preview of the text helps them feel comfortable with the mass of information they are about to start consuming. Letting them use technology tools like audiobooks and ebooks gives them a bit more control over how they're inputting information and relieves some of the burden of having to both read long stretches of text and comprehend all the details coming at them. Graphic novels can help give them mental pictures of the material while allowing them to compare the original text to the shortened, pictorial version. And teaching students to make connections to themselves or things outside of the story helps them feel more related to the text.

It may take some deep consideration on your part, but with a student who just can't connect to the material, it's worth brainstorming to see if you can find that entry point.

And yes, now when I go to Shakespeare shows, I do some prep beforehand. Sometimes I watch a few clips on YouTube or read a plot summary, and if I have enough warning, I go to the library or bookstore to find the graphic novel version. This way, I can actually stay awake when I see Shakespeare, so when people in the lobby ask me if I enjoyed the show, I no longer have to fake enthusiasm!

CHAPTER 6

TEACH IN HIGH DEFINITION
How to Make Things Clear Visually

Disneyland can be a wonderful place, no doubt. But I also find it overwhelming.

When I walk through the park, there is so much competing for my senses that I feel anxious. I certainly cannot give my friends my full attention, that's for sure. My head and eyes dart around trying to process all of it at once. Can you imagine trying to read a book in Disneyland? Or solve quadratic equations?

Disneyland isn't the only time I feel this way. Crowded airports, the subway, sports bars that have lots of TVs hanging on the walls, and typical indoor shopping malls are all places I get overwhelmed due to the amount of stimuli in the environment. At some point the thought hits me that perhaps, for our attention challenged students, it might feel something like this in our classrooms every day.

There are a lot of stimuli in any given classroom: fifteen to thirty-five other kids, work samples on the walls, a library full of books, that super cool Harry Potter poster at the back of the room, other colorful posters with rules or inspirational phrases on them, the mailbox area and homework bins for ingoing and outgoing assignments, backpacks, supplies, and so on. When we teach, we're competing with our own environment.

Here's another factor to consider. We live in an HD society. High definition. We are all looking at screens more and more each day, and young people have grown up in a world where they have a great deal of information presented to them in high-definition clarity. TVs, phones, computers, and tablets all present bright, clear, extremely detailed imagery and visual information. These devices are engineered to draw and sustain viewers' attention to the screen.

So how can we, as teachers, keep students focused on our teaching and assignments for seven hours a day in our classrooms, especially when students are so used to digesting crystal clear digital input that is a foot from their faces?

We have to make our own classroom into a high-definition environment for learning. This does not mean turning your classroom into a Best Buy showroom, though some technology will certainly be involved.

For starters, keep your room tidy, well-organized, and easy to navigate; nothing should be too difficult to locate. Of course, you may want some pictures on the wall purely for decoration, and you obviously need posters and signs to section off the room and highlight key components of your class, but try to avoid posters with a significant amount of text that may overwhelm students. There's a fine line between your room looking like a fun, organized place and looking like a carnival or a train station terminal with information everywhere you turn.

Preferential seating is a standard support for students with attention challenges. Typically, we seat students with distractibility at the front of the room, and this often works well, though I have seen students in these seats turn around compulsively to check out the stimuli behind them. If this happens, you could try the back of the room, but then they're far from the action. You'll have to adjust accordingly.

> If we hope to draw in students and keep their attention, our material not only has to be interesting, it has to be clear: high-definition clarity.

But beyond decorating properly and adjusting seating locations, what can we do to help students sift through the room's stimuli to focus on what's really important?

If we hope to draw in students and keep their attention, our material not only has to be interesting, it has to be clear. I'm talking high-definition clarity. And again, we don't necessarily need technology to accomplish this.

Just some simple, practical tools and supports.

Color-Code for Clarity

Color-coding can be an effective way to help students make connections, recognize patterns, and comprehend material. Color can often make ideas clear to students when the words or numbers themselves may be confusing. And when connections, patterns, and ideas are clear to students, they'll probably be quicker to access the material.

Color-coding is a natural fit when teaching phonics patterns, word families, and prefixes and suffixes in the early grades, especially with students who are showing difficulty with beginning reading skills, whether due to attention or decoding issues. Color-coding specific patterns makes it easier for students to cue in to phonics rules and word parts. For kindergartners, it may be as simple as making the consonants one color and the vowels another, even with simple C-V-C words. When teaching affixes, make prefixes green and suffixes red within complete words. When I start teaching students multisyllabic words, I'll use colors to make the separate syllables stand out. For students with attention challenges, this helps them engage with the decoding process and may help them recognize patterns quicker. Of course, the idea is that you phase this out slowly so students can generalize the skills to reading typical black type.

In math, I color-code constantly, even for seemingly simple operations. For example, when first teaching kindergartners to oscillate between solving addition and subtraction problems, I make the + and – signs different colors to add another way for them to instantly discriminate between the operations.

Multiple-step operations like multi-digit multiplication can be seriously confusing to some of our students. It requires working memory, sustained mental energy, and organization, not to mention knowing multiplication facts. I can imagine how a long division problem looks to a student with executive function challenges or dyslexia. Like a word search puzzle with numbers! Word search puzzles can make me nauseous but imagine if they were color-coded. Maybe the consonants were blue, and the vowels were orange. That would help me immensely by giving a bit of clarity to the jumble of letters. I try to generalize this approach whenever I teach multistep problems that include various operations.

So for multi-digit multiplication, use color-coding to help clarify the steps and help students better encode the processes into memory. Start by making each digit of the bottom numbers a different color. For example, in 347 x 26, make the tens number blue (the 2) and the ones number red (the 6). Start modeling the procedures by multiplying the 6 by the three digits above. Draw a red line from the 6 to the 7 and put the corresponding product down below, also in red (42). Of course, put the 2 below the equals line and regroup the 4 over the next digit in the top number (the 4). Proceed like this until you've multiplied the 6 by each digit of the top number, all done in red.

Then do the same for the tens digit (the 2), all in blue.

Use a third color, purple perhaps, to add them up to find the final product.

The results look like the example to the right.

Of course, there are different ways of completing multi-digit multiplication, but whichever way you teach, you can use color-coding to help students see exactly how to move through the steps of the operation solely through the color patterns. It takes what once looked like a jumble of numbers and multiplication operations and gives them a sense of visual organization: red represents multiplying the ones digit of the bottom number, and blue represents the tens digit. Obviously, it doesn't really matter which colors you choose, just that the colors give some extra visual organization to the problem. To reinforce this further, have students use colored pencils and mimic this sort of color-coding while they're first attempting problems. The idea is that after using colors for a while, they can phase out the colors and try problems without the visual support.

$$\begin{array}{r} {\scriptstyle 2}\;\;{\scriptstyle 4} \\ \mathbf{347} \\ \times\,\mathbf{26} \\ \hline \mathbf{2082} \\ \mathbf{694x} \\ \hline \mathbf{9022} \end{array}$$

Use this technique with any sort of problems with multiple operations. For example, when teaching the steps for long division, use a different color for each step. You may already know the "Dad, Mother, Sister, Brother" mnemonic for recalling the steps, standing for "Divide, Multiply, Subtract, Bring Down." When demonstrating moving through the steps, make the divide step one color, effectively making all of the numbers in the quotient up top one color (let's say green). For the multiply step, put the product in a different color under the dividend (could be red). Next, when you subtract, choose a third color for the answer. And then when you bring down the next digit of the dividend, make that number a fourth color. As you start the cycle again, use those same colors for the steps. Start off with green for division.

It may seem antithetical to have students with attention challenges use four different colored pencils to complete a problem; isn't that just putting more pressure on their executive functions? It might. If you find this is the case with a particular student, just use the colors yourself as you model the problem for them and give them a printed out reference copy of a long division problem completed with the color-coding. On the other hand, I've seen lots of students for whom using different colored pencils helps engage them to the multiple steps. It slows them down a bit, but this is a good thing. It makes them consider the individual steps and check in with themselves to make sure they're completing the proper step at the right moment.

The idea is to make the different steps in these problems pop out visually, making it easier for students to see the pattern of operations and how it repeats. This concept transfers naturally to other skills such as reading and processing information.

ATTENTION GRABBER
Clearing Up the Colonies

Isaiah, a fifth-grade student on the spectrum who I was working with after school, was an enthusiastic learner with a great memory for facts and figures but information needed to be presented to him clearly. With his attention and executive function challenges, he had difficulty organizing information on his own, and as a result, he wasn't really making sense of what he read or using analysis and evaluation. I also knew he had the potential to process visual information, because I'd seen him play *Super Mario Bros.* online, and he was a whiz at avoiding Koopa Troopas!

Isaiah had an upcoming test that required the memorization of a glut of information about the original American colonies. The information told about the similarities and differences of three regions: New England colonies, Middle colonies, and Southern colonies. In class, he was able to take notes along with his classmates, both copying information the teacher had written on the board and adding some things she said verbally. His notes appeared in outline form with headings for each group of colonies and information listed as numbered entries.

But when I asked him what he knew about the different colonies, he didn't remember anything from class. As we began to read the information and attempt to memorize it, he struggled to encode it into his memory, and he wasn't able to recognize any patterns or connections across the information. In this case, it was simply too much information with too many variables, including three different sections of colonies and all sorts of facts about colonial life. His mental energy was draining quickly.

I noticed that the information about the colonies he had typed into an outline all fell into three categories: *religion, farming/food,* and *economy*. The problem was that the facts weren't organized in this way. After discussing this with him, I took out three highlighters of different colors and showed him how to use each color to highlight a different category. We chose yellow for religion, orange for farming/food, and pink for economy.

Now we had information presented under subheadings (colony groups) and within those, facts were color-coded to make it clear there were three main categories of information.

Immediately, this new organization and clarity led to a conversation about religion in colonial America. Isaiah told me how the Puritans came to the New World for religious freedom, and we then compared how each group of colonies had a different approach to that very freedom. It was easy to see because the religion information, though scattered between the three colony groups, was now highlighted in yellow, making it easier for Isaiah to compare and contrast them.

Isaiah was starting to show engagement and interest in the material.

Use Graphic Organizers

During a given school day, students have to absorb a ton of new information. A good amount of that is usually presented on the whiteboard, on paper, or in books. It's challenging for students with attention deficits to ingest and comprehend lots of written language for a sustained amount of time.

Graphic organizers are visual frames and charts that help our brains process chunks of information by organizing it by its meanings and implications, emphasizing the key ideas. Bubble maps, T-charts, flow maps, pie charts, character maps, and semantic maps each have their own specific uses to match the type of information being presented. For our students with difficulties inputting information, these can help them do so while organizing it properly in their memory. It's like organizing a closet. The pants are hanging to the left. Shirts to the right. Tank tops in the top drawer of the dresser. Socks, second drawer. Now, when you need to get dressed in a hurry, you know where everything is. And because these charts present information in a clear, organized frame, it can be easier for students to sustain focus on them.

So, while many students can just study outlines or lists of information and memorize the information regardless of how it's organized, our students with challenges are often better served using a graphic organizer as a study guide. Graphic organizers are a well-established teaching support most teachers employ regularly, but you can take these basic tools further by using them more aggressively with your students who really need them. Use them whenever you can, either when you're presenting information on the whiteboard or when you're giving handouts to help students prepare for quizzes and tests.

ATTENTION GRABBER
Clearing Up the Colonies (continued)

My student Isaiah (page 143) had his notes color-coded by categories of information, and he was making progress, but he was still having difficulty memorizing the information and drawing connections. Though the information was laid out in an outline format, and each colony group's information—about religion, farming/food, and economy—was color-coded, the information appeared distant on the page from the categories it compared to. There was simply too much information just listed on the page.

I needed to take the clarity of this study guide up a notch.

At this point, I suggested we make a graphic organizer. Using PowerPoint, we created a typical table with columns and rows. The top row had the three colony groups—New England, Middle, and Southern—as the heads of the columns. Each row would give the corresponding information for each colony group related to religion, farming/food, and economy.

Isaiah looked at his notes, easily used the color-coding to search out the information by topic, and typed the information into the organizer. First, he found the facts highlighted in yellow and filled in the three different religious approaches for the three colony groups. Next, he looked for the orange farming/food information and wrote those into the organizer. Last, he found the pink highlighted information about the economies and transcribed that into the organizer.

An important point here: This may seem super obvious, but you don't need a computer to make a graphic organizer for your students. What I did with Isaiah, you can create instantly on your whiteboard for the whole class. The drawback is that it's going to be erased pretty darn soon because math class is next. Wasn't part of the point to create a study guide for your students to take home?

Two solutions.

One, have the students take a blank piece of paper and quickly draw the organizer as you have. Then they can fill in the correct information.

Two, the much easier way: Take out your phone and snap a picture. Email it to yourself, and then you can print it out for any students who want it. Or if your students have phones, they can take the picture themselves.

By the way, after studying the graphic organizer of information, Isaiah could tell me all the information, no problem. He was totally ready for that test.

Use Pictures and Symbols

Pictures really can be worth a thousand words, especially to students. Sometimes, with skills or concepts that require a lot of reading or processing, an image or symbol can quickly guide students' eyes and help them encode something into memory and/or make an idea clear so that the sight of it later helps them retrieve the stored information.

ATTENTION GRABBER
Blending Letters into a Smoothie

As a resource teacher, I taught reading to groups of students with dyslexia and/or attention challenges. For some of these students, having the combination of these two challenges made it extremely difficult to learn new phonics patterns and, consequently, improve fluency. Sustaining mental energy during our thirty-minute sessions was challenging enough for most of them, but even within the reading of a single sentence, you could see the fatigue as students had to remember all the phonics rules they'd learned and know when to apply them (let's not even get into how often English breaks its common phonics patterns).

One of my groups of first and second graders consisted of English language learners who had first learned Spanish. For these students, even basic skills like blending two consonants could take weeks or even months to learn, develop, and master. I was constantly looking for new and better ways to engage them. Emilia, a student who always came to my group with a smile, could only sustain focus on my lessons for about a minute, and her reading was not improving. One day, I got the idea to equate letter "blending" with "blending smoothies" or *licuados*. When I first taught the skill, I asked students if they liked *licuados* and which two fruits were their favorite ingredients; Emilia was especially excited to talk about which flavors she enjoyed. I pointed out that the flavors in smoothies are blended, but you taste both of them, and that's the way it is with blending letters: You say the sounds of *both* letters. To help them recall the concept of blending, I had a picture of a blended smoothie on the whiteboard that they could reference if needed. They would then examine the two letters and make the two sounds. "Now put them in the blender," I'd say, or I'd just point to the picture of the smoothie.

Emilia was more engaged in this particular skill than she'd been with any of my other phonics lessons. The skill remained a challenge for her and the others—some mastered the skill quicker—but the image/concept kept them interested so they could keep practicing each day I saw them. Sometimes they would even come to class and tell me about the real smoothie they had the previous day. It was just a little picture, but it communicated a set of reading rules in an instant.

I try to include images or symbols in my teaching as often as I can. I've used a little cartoon of a detective with a magnifying glass to help students engage with the skill of making inferences: "Use the clues!" You can use the images of a car and an elevator to engage students in moving along x and y coordinates: Car goes left and right; the elevator goes up and down. Or use the image of dollar bills along with quarters, dimes, nickels, and pennies as visual cues to remind students about the meaning of decimals and place values: dollars, or whole numbers, are to the left of the decimal, and the coins totaling under one whole (dollar) are written to the right of the decimal.

Anytime you think of it, try to include pictures or symbols in your lessons to stand in for chunks of information or complicated concepts.

Emphasize Key Words

I don't think people read emails with the attention they used to. It happens too often that people miss information I put in emails, and they write back with confusion. And to be honest, sometimes I miss information because I, too, am skimming my emails. So I've developed strategies. Now when I send emails, I use **bold** and *italics*, and sometimes a ***combination of both***, to emphasize the key words and ideas I want the receiver of the email to focus on. Honestly, I wish people did this for me.

Emphasizing key words with visual cues like bold, italics, underlining, or highlighting draws attention to them. This can be useful for students looking at worksheets. Even if the directions are straightforward and relatively brief, it may be worth highlighting the key words in the directions and questions. Consider a worksheet that says, "Read the following passage and write down the verbs that end in –ing and the adverbs that end in –ly." You could highlight the key elements they have to look for: "Read the following passage and write down the **verbs that end in –*ing*** and the **adverbs that end in –*ly*.**" Just circling or highlighting these words will draw the students' attention to the key directions, when otherwise they may be resistant to even starting.

The same sort of technique can be done if you have questions written on the whiteboard, by underlining or circling the key words or phrases you want students to focus on. Also, if you're showing students something on the computer, whether you're online or in any sort of word processing program, you can always click and drag over words to highlight them. When I read online articles with students, I highlight key ideas as we're reading so that we can discuss them during a pause, or I may highlight a specific piece of text I want the students to focus on.

Highlighting can also be a helpful tool to emphasize key information in subjects like history and social studies when middle school students have to read long, dense passages in textbooks or photocopied packets. Empower students to highlight phrases and sentences that they think are the key points; teach them that often, the first and last sentences of a paragraph tell you the main idea. Encourage them to also highlight things they find interesting.

Afterward, when they look at the passage, they can use the high-lighted, emphasized information as a guide to the key ideas.

Reduce Visual Clutter on Worksheets

This issue comes up a lot in math. I often see workbooks and pages that don't provide nearly enough room for the student to perform all the necessary operations. Why do they make double-digit regrouping problems so small? Why do they leave so little room above and below the problem? Sure, some of our students naturally write small or have the ability to do so without expending much mental effort. For them, these sheets aren't a big hindrance.

Our students with attention deficits aren't as fortunate. For them, it may be much more difficult to write small, use space efficiently, and attend to work that's difficult for them to navigate visually.

Name:_____ Date:_____

48 ×80	97 ×23	15 ×97	39 ×27	28 ×50
73 ×54	57 ×57	60 ×95	76 ×60	26 ×36
57 ×38	71 ×38	31 ×25	75 ×47	63 ×59
10 ×96	86 ×69	32 ×81	33 ×84	99 ×82
85 ×19	95 ×75	28 ×83	87 ×80	39 ×27
69 ×13	20 ×91	14 ×96	16 ×75	71 ×38
90 ×38	83 ×12	50 ×30	27 ×47	26 ×36

Name:_____ Date:_____

48 × 80	97 × 23	15 × 97	39 × 27
28 × 50	73 × 54	57 × 57	60 × 95
76 × 60	26 × 36	57 × 38	71 × 38

Some of the same issues come up with language arts worksheets as well. So what sort of fast, easy fixes can we do?

- **Draw lines between problems/questions.** This is a simple, quick fix. Before giving quizzes to students, draw straight lines to create boxes around individual problems. This helps make clear delineations between the problems and gives each problem its own little piece of real estate. For language arts, history, or science sheets with lots of questions on them, section off questions using straight lines across the page.

- **Provide separate, premade answer sheets.** Take a blank sheet and draw lines on it to create nice, big boxes; size them depending on how much room you think the students will need to work out the answer. Number the boxes to correspond to the quiz, test, or worksheet questions. Now, instead of having to cram their work onto the quiz pages, students can simply use the answer sheet and do the work in the corresponding box. You should model for them how to line up the answer sheet with the worksheet in such a way that it puts the question on the worksheet they're currently working on right

next to the corresponding box on the answer sheet. They don't have to rewrite the problem; they can simply start working it out in the blank space of the corresponding box. You can also teach students to circle their final answer. These pages not only give students enough space to work out the problems, but by putting each problem in a separate box, they also isolate the problems for students visually.

- **Cover up the nearby problems/questions on the page.** You can do this with whatever is handy: a blank sheet of paper, pencil box, folder, whatever. I use sticky notes all the time when trying to make pages less visually cluttered for my students—not just for math but for anything they're reading—and it is very easy to teach students to do this for themselves. Moving the sticky notes around as they progress through the problems may keep them engaged with the work, although they could also get sidetracked and turn the sticky notes into a little game. If the sticky notes are too distracting, just redirect them to use the answer sheet for the same purpose.

- **Enlarge the print.** If you have the worksheet in a Word doc, make the font big. Go to at least 16 points, but I say it can't be too big. We're so accustomed to reading 12-point type that it seems natural to have our worksheets in this size as well, but if we magnify the words and numbers for our students, the page looks like it's in HD! If you don't have the worksheet as a digital file but just a hard copy, you can throw the sheet on the photocopy machine and enlarge it, even just a little bit.

A co-teacher and I were tasked with giving end-of-unit math quizzes to our group of students with learning and attention challenges. All of the second-grade teachers gave the same quizzes so that their progress could be tracked uniformly throughout the program as the students moved through the grades.

For our students, the quizzes were very difficult to navigate due to clutter and other issues: limited room for work and answers, difficulty delineating between problems, small type, and so on. On the first couple of quizzes, we noticed these things affecting our students' performances—many of them had questions about where they should do their work and where they should write their answers. Overall, students seemed thrown by the pages themselves. We looked around the room, and many students were disengaging from the quiz, even when they knew how to do the operations.

When we started applying adjustments to make the quizzes look HD, our students became more engaged with the problems, and we didn't need to redirect them as often. These supports don't solve the problems for them—they still have to learn the procedures and skills—but they do help kids remain attentive to the tasks by making the pages more clear and easier to navigate visually.

Give Models of Expected Work

Imagine having to put together an IKEA cube organizer without pictures to go with the instructions. Step-by-step, you have to *read* the directions, not knowing what the completed table or cabinet even looks like at the end. Doesn't sound fun, does it?

Models help us visualize how our work is expected to look.

For bigger projects that require any sort of building or crafts, most teachers show a completed project from a previous year. In California, students usually study the Spanish Missions at some point in elementary school. Often, a creative project serves as the culmination: making a brochure, a poster, or even an entire model of one of the settlements. Showcasing a completed project from previous years helps students visualize what their own projects are expected to look like.

I would go a step further for students who typically have difficulty with multistep assignments, especially if the project you're assigning has any sort of design and/or construction element to it. Let's say it's a project where students have to invent and make a board game with Renaissance artists as the theme. Assuming you have a completed project from a previous year—even a board game with a different theme—bring it in. Or, if students keep their projects, snap a few pictures of the game board from multiple angles and any cards or props included before returning them to students. The next year you can show these images to students and even print them, so students can take them home. Having these images at home may give them a more tangible end point to aim for.

This strategy applies to any type of assignment, even if it's a seemingly simple cut, paste, and color project you're giving your kindergartners or first graders. For example, if you're having students color and then cut out turkey pieces to paste into a whole Thanksgiving bird, consider which students usually lose engagement during multiple-step processes like these and put a completed turkey on those students' tables, right in front of them. Encourage the students to check in with the model step-by-step to see if they're on track.

Of course, as you explain the project and show the models, be clear about what aspects of the project are a "must do" and which are open to interpretation. That way, students have the opportunity to conjure their creativity to make projects their own, even if they use a model to help them focus on the finished product.

If you'd rather not use models so intensively for the whole class because you're worried that everyone's project will end up too similar, do a limited showcase of work models during recess for students who have shown engagement challenges with longer projects.

Another area to consider using models for is writing projects. Let's say you want your students to write a solid ten-sentence paragraph comparing two characters from a novel. You want students to have a thesis statement, two quotes from the text that help defend their thesis, and some explanation to make sure their argument is clear. For students with production issues, it's probably not enough to just give them this prompt and let them work.

Instead, provide a model of the end product so they can see what your expectation *looks* like. Obviously, you can't give them a model from which they can just copy the sentences; we want them to think about their own ideas. But our students with production issues will really benefit from *seeing* the structure, content, and length of the writing you're looking for—literally the size and shape of the paragraph. Having the visual reference will act like a map to them. If it's multiple paragraphs, the kids will be able to see what the shape of a multi-paragraph essay looks like and how big the paragraphs should be.

The bottom line is, don't assume the student can instantly visualize what you're talking about when you describe the project with words. Models give students a clear goal to aim for and may keep them engaged through the various steps to get there. I can think of more than a few times I would have given up on constructing that IKEA bookshelf if I didn't have pictures of it in front of me.

Project Digitally

And here we come full circle to the technical meaning of the words *high definition*. For students who are consistently inattentive during lessons, digital projection can be a very effective tool in helping to jump-start their input controls.

Document cameras allow you to write on a worksheet on your desk and have it projected large and clear in real time. You can zoom in, affect the brightness, and even create a still image. Having things projected big and bright at the front of the room is a huge attention getter. And I've observed that when teachers interact with the projected images by using highlighters or even just their forefingers, it draws students' eyes. I think one of the reasons it works is because students have such positive associations with digital interfaces.

ATTENTION GRABBER
HD Reading Group

My co-teacher and I were conducting a reading group for second-grade students with significant reading and attention challenges. One of the first books we read with them was from the Mr. Putter & Tabby series. We started out the year having students follow along in their own books, but too many of them could not sustain their focus on the pages in front of them and would require constant redirection to help them find the place, even as we read slowly. It was too difficult for us to run around the room helping different students keep their place at different times. One girl in particular, Sage, really couldn't sustain engagement with the book at all.

We had only used the document projector to help model writing and other skills, but not yet for reading. During the next reading session, we placed the book underneath the projector so that the page was now displayed big and bright on the whiteboard at the front of the room. This way, students had the option to just look up at the digital image where the words were large and clear. Either my co-teacher or I would hold a pointer and use it like a finger, pointing to the words as we read. We also decided to call up students to the board to hold the pointer to the words.

Guess which student we called up first.

Sage came up and held that pointer proudly, acting like the teacher, and she was able to keep it moving to match the words she was hearing about how Mr. Putter and Tabby's neighbor hurt her leg and needed someone to help out with her dog. After she returned to her seat and we called up others to hold the pointer, Sage showed more spark in her ability to sustain focus on the text. We reminded her, and the rest of the class, that if they didn't want to look at their books, they could follow along with the projected image on the board.

We noticed an immediate improvement in how many of the students would sustain engagement with the book during our lessons. About half of the class preferred looking up at the board. Of course, we still had to give them personal reminders, at times, to refocus on the book or the board, but the projected image of the pages clearly reduced the number of times per lesson we had to do so. The kids loved the story, and I remember them all laughing especially hard when Mr. Putter and Tabby tried to take the crazy dog for a walk.

Just having a projector to use with your laptop can be helpful as well. You can search the internet for pictures and information, create slide shows, or watch videos on sites like BrainPOP, all while projecting it on your whiteboard so the whole class can see it.

GUEST SPEAKER
BRIAN JULIAN

Brian Julian has taught chess for more than seven years in one-to-one settings, enrichment classes, and alternative schools. His philosophy is "Chess for Everyone," and he uses the game to help students work through specific learning, social, and developmental issues. Here he tells a story about how he engaged nonverbal students on the spectrum through visual supports.

Recently, I was asked to teach a class of six students on the spectrum at an alternative school. All had severe verbal communication issues, with some using text-to-speech apps and others barely speaking by any means. I was excited by the challenge but also a bit intimidated. Would I be able to communicate to them how to play this complex game?

I showed them how the pieces move using an actual game set, but the students couldn't remember the different pieces' movements, nor did they understand that they had choices, all of which suggested that they were not *seeing* the board and pieces clearly. Chess is already a busy game visually, but with this unique group of students I really had to think outside the "square"!

The first thing I tried was using the big whiteboard at the front of the room. Without the distraction and clutter of the chessboard, I wrote each piece's name nice and big on the board (these students, though nonverbal, could read well) and drew arrows showing how each piece could move. After this support, I saw some of the students became more accurate with moving their pieces when we practiced on actual boards.

But during actual game play, many of the students struggled to see the different spaces a given piece could move to. So I had each student download the free game Chess Prime 3D onto their tablets. When it was their turn, they would see a 3D model of the board in the app, and it highlighted for them the possible squares they could move to. The students were immediately engaged by the interface, and once they made the move on the tablet, they could easily translate that move with pieces on the physical board.

One particular student, Sebastian, still couldn't understand his choices for possible moves and was just moving his pieces without any thought. His aide suddenly got inspired, grabbed a ruler, and we improvised a new strategy. Once Sebastian selected a piece for his turn, I would lay the ruler on the board showing one of that piece's possible trajectories. Then I would use another ruler to show another option, adding more rulers as needed. This student would then consider the choices and select a path that made sense to help him win. With the rulers helping him see his possible moves, Sebastian finally became more engaged with the game.

After a few weeks, as students grew more comfortable with the game rules, they actually began having conversations with one another through their text-to-speech apps about the game itself! I've learned that for any students who struggle to connect with the game, it helps to teach them the same exact information multiple times—how the pieces move, how they have choices, and so on—presenting it in as many different ways as I can come up with.

Anyone teaching any sort of subject, skill, or art form is confronted with obstacles in how to transmit information clearly. Brian's specific circumstances, though unique, show how bringing visual clarity to teaching can be crucial in engagement and comprehension. And his techniques are transferrable as well. If you have a tablet available, search for apps that may bring clarity to a confusing topic. I've used phonics apps that are colorful and fun to use along with apps for different math domains like place value and fractions.

And Brian's use of the ruler to show the trajectories of game pieces is a simple, quick solution that he improvised on the spot. Any time you're using hands-on math materials, consider if there's a quick adjustment that would make the concept that much more clear.

The Big Takeaway

For students with attention challenges, processing visual information for sustained periods in classrooms can be extremely challenging. It's like walking through an amusement park or carnival and trying to be attentive to just one thing. The park may be a wonderful place with lots to offer, but for some people (like me), it is difficult to be there for long periods of time; I get overwhelmed by the stimuli and can't really stay engaged with all of it, and sometimes I just want to get the heck out of there.

When we want students to focus on something, it should be crystal clear. Clutter is our enemy. Nothing should be vague. Using color-coding and highlighters to emphasize key pieces of information is very easy to do and can be effective in making things more clear. Try sticky notes or index cards to block unneeded information, allowing students to narrow their focus. Use graphic organizers to make key pieces of information distinct in a frame that also brings clarity to how pieces of information are related to each other. Provide models of expected work for students to have in the classroom, at their seat, or to take home so they can visualize the expected product. And if you have access to projection technology, look for creative ways to use it, especially when engagement is particularly lacking with students.

Kids are used to all their media being in high definition. Let's try to make all our classroom work be in high def as well.

CHAPTER 7

ADJUST THEIR MIRROR
How to Encourage Self-Awareness and Self-Management

Self-awareness is like a mirror. It's a reflective tool that most people carry around all the time. It allows us to see our own behavior and recognize if what we're doing is acceptable to us and those around us. If something isn't going well for us—maybe we're late on bills, our house is getting messy, we're getting into more arguments than usual—we tend to notice (most of the time, anyway). It's an innate ability we don't think about; it just works for us. We're consistently engaged with our self-perception, our relationship to our current environment, our obligations, and the people around us.

But for students with attention deficits, self-awareness may not be innate. It's difficult for them to recognize when they're being impulsive, doing something bothersome to others, or being socially inappropriate. It may be even harder for them to be aware of their own inattentiveness or mental energy levels.

These students need help in developing that mirror.

Back in the introduction of this book, you had the opportunity to look at your own strengths and deficits with attention (page 10). Maybe you struggle to stay focused when reading a novel. Maybe you check Twitter every time you get stuck in a writing project, and those check-ins wind up taking an hour or more. Maybe, like me, your mind drifts while you're driving and you end up missing an exit (or three). Thinking about our own attention profiles does more than just help us empathize with students. It also gives us self-awareness so we can redirect ourselves when needed. In short, we're more engaged.

Helping students develop self-awareness enables them to employ a *quality check* over their behaviors, which could result in more engagement as they learn to take control of their impulsivity and help steer their own attention functions.

In my years doing applied behavior analysis (ABA) with students with autism and ADHD, I learned how to design and implement self-monitoring systems. These typically involve the teacher, behavior specialist, and student agreeing to target a specific behavior to extinguish and replace with a new behavior and creating a formal system by which the student checks in with his or her own progress and receives some form of positive reinforcement. One major component of shaping students' behavior is the use of visual cues and tools to give reminders and bring self-awareness to students about their behaviors.

That is the focus of this chapter: how you can easily and quickly create visual cues along with other inexpensive, simple tools that engage the student and help adjust that student's mirror. These tools

Helping students develop self-awareness enables them to employ a *quality check* over their behaviors, resulting in more engagement as they take control of their impulsivity and steer their own attention functions.

could come in the form of cue cards, charts, organizers, or other practical tools. Clearly, these sorts of supports have to be age-appropriate; for example, an older student may not want a reminder chart on his or her desk for all to see.

As I've said elsewhere in the book, if you have students who display significant behavioral challenges—oppositional defiance, aggressiveness, self-harm—or conditions related to their social-emotional or psychological well-being, more intensive interventions need to be implemented in collaboration with any mental health professionals who may be treating the student.

This chapter focuses on the everyday classroom/academic tasks that require self-awareness and other executive functions: impulse control, quality checks, awareness of one's mental energy, time management, planning ahead, and organization.

Controlling Impulses

Most of us possess the self-control needed to maintain socially acceptable behavior, but for students with ADHD hyperactive-impulsive type, or students with related executive function challenges, this may be their toughest hurdle. Controlling impulses includes multiple self-regulation functions like being able to stop in the heat of a moment and shift focus, inhibit oneself, foresee possible consequences of our actions, and identify possible alternative choices and make one of those choices.

Impulsivity can take many forms throughout a student's school day, both socially and academically. In the classroom, these behaviors are often disruptive to the individual as well as peers and the teacher. They include excessive social talking during lessons, calling out either on- or off-topic comments, saying inappropriate things, and more physical behaviors that may arise from frustration such as crumpling up a worksheet, yelling, or running out of the room.

Certainly, step one is to remind these students about appropriate behavior in the classroom, discuss why their impulsive behavior is disruptive, and brainstorm alternative behaviors. The reality is that one conversation is not going to suddenly rewire their executive functioning. And if we're just reprimanding and scolding them every day, it results in a strained teacher-student relationship while also diminishing their self-esteem. Chapter 2 addresses reinforcement systems, particularly with regard to building confidence, but outside of marble jars and class currencies, other tools can help students gain self-awareness of their behaviors.

Cue cards are little personalized reminders—around the size of an index card—students can keep at their desks that give them a visual cue for the target behavior. You could use an image from online or sketch something out. The idea is that the image will serve as a quick, instant reminder of

HANDS TO SELF

the improper impulsive action and/or the replacement behavior. For example, for students who struggle to keep their hands off of peers during lineup time, you could put a picture of students standing in line with their arms at their sides; or maybe even have your student pose in that position, snap a pic, and put that on a card.

Consult with the students to see which image they feel will be the most potent reminder. Older students can take the lead on what sort of reminder they think may be helpful—perhaps it's not a cue card at all but an object they may keep on their person that gives them a similar reminder.

One of the most common behaviors for students with impulse control challenges is to call out.

Often.

Right in the middle of class.

It can be terribly frustrating when attempting to control this. Telling students over and over again to "Raise your hand!" doesn't typically have a lasting effect. The behavior will not improve until the student can recognize his or her own struggle with restraint. This is another situation where using a student's interests can be a huge help to you.

ATTENTION GRABBER
Raise That Hand, Says SpongeBob

Isabel was a third grader who never raised her hand, not to answer or ask questions, even when she needed help. But she did have a lot to say and often had an interesting perspective on things. She also would blurt out comments or questions in the middle of lessons that were on topic but disruptive to the lesson's flow nonetheless.

I thought that a visual reminder card would help, but I needed to capture her attention with it. Rather than make a generic "Raise Your Hand" card, I searched for images on the web of her favorite character, SpongeBob SquarePants, with his hand raised. (I was fortunate to find one, but if you can't find a picture of the character doing the specific gesture, just grab another image of the character and add a speech bubble with the direction, along with a generic raised hand.) I usually tape the picture underneath the word cue and then laminate it, but you can just glue the picture onto an index card and write the words above it.

The cue card was kept either on her desk or in her open-topped pencil case, and at the beginning of lessons, I would point to it as an extra reminder for her. In the ensuing weeks, she listened to her square-shaped hero and began raising her hand more frequently to ask relevant questions and add ideas to our discussions.

When we teach replacement behaviors, it's important to reinforce the new actions with either verbal praise or a fulfillment of the function of the behavior. Isabel would get impulses to speak out and have everyone's focus on her. When she started raising her hand to do so, it was key that I called on her so that she could recognize the merit in doing it.

The card served as a visual reminder for her about the expected replacement behavior for calling out. After a couple of weeks, I stopped referencing the cue card, and she probably stopped looking at it as well. Eventually, the new behavior became part of her repertoire, and the visual cue was no longer needed.

There is always the risk that the card results in the student using the replacement behavior *too* frequently. In the case of Isabel, there were times when she would raise her hand almost compulsively; it was like she was trading one impulse for another. In this situation, it was a fine line between calling on her enough to reinforce the positive behavior but not call on her too much so as to reinforce the impulsivity of her hand raising. ABA practitioners use different reinforcement schedules, including fixed ratio, where you reinforce every time the wanted behavior occurs, or variable ratio, where you may reinforce every two or three times, mixing it up.

I try to start with fixed ratio and phase into variable ratio. In other words, I initially called on her every time she raised her hand, but then only half the time she raised her hand, and then maybe a third of the time. In a sense, you're trying to figure out how many times you *cannot* call on a student before she loses faith in the replacement behavior and, essentially, our agreement that if she raises her hand, she'll usually get to speak.

Another important point is that it's not realistic to expect students with impulsivity to act perfectly at all times. Occasionally, Isabel would give in to impulse and call out. It's bound to happen. Usually, just a quick point to the cue card will bring a student right back to recalling how to control the impulse.

> When you support a student's new self-management behavior, reinforce it early and often. Students should immediately see the benefits of the new behavior.

Older students who are socially conscious probably won't want this sort of kid-friendly reminder on their desks, so what's an alternative tool? You could give them a stack of sticky notes and encourage them to jot down quickly whatever they want to say, wait for an appropriate time, and then raise their hand to share. The stickies, like the visual cue card, help bring self-awareness to their impulse control and serve as a reminder that sits on the desk.

When you support a new self-management behavior, reinforce it early and often. Students should immediately see the benefits of the new behavior. If they raise their hand, call on them! Over time, scale back the reinforcement, easing them into the rotation among other hand raisers.

Quality Checks

When we write emails or reports for work, we always look them over before sending and submitting. We want to make sure we're presenting our ideas or work in a clear and organized manner, and maybe more importantly, we want to exhibit our best selves to the world. This applies to social situations as well. We take time to decide what to wear. We groom ourselves meticulously. We spend time looking in mirrors. And when we interact with people, we are constantly checking in with ourselves to make sure we're being socially appropriate. If we happen to say something that may have offended someone, we recognize it and apologize (ideally), and we are consequently more careful with our words in the future.

These sorts of self-checks in the quality of our social presentation and—in the context of this book—of our work production, are very difficult for students with attention challenges. It's a set of skills we can help them develop by targeting specific situations when they should be doing a quality check, which might be during and/or after work production.

Chapter 4 addresses messy writing with typing and voice recognition, but there are often shorter assignments, worksheets, and so on, when students have to quickly write down ideas. Of course, we know just telling students to write neater may help a little bit, but ultimately they won't internalize the self-management this way; they'll most likely keep coming back to you after minor adjustments and ask, "Is this neat enough?"

Handwriting is another area where occupational therapists can support students, but what can teachers do to help students be more aware of the illegibility of their work and develop the self-awareness to give it a quality check? As with impulse control, cue cards and other visual reminders can help.

ATTENTION GRABBER
Land Letters on the Runway

Oscar was a second grader with attention deficits whose letters were oversized, drifting above the lines, and dropping below them. There were some fine motor skills issues there, and an occupational therapist had met with Oscar a couple of times, but it was evident he also was rushing and wasn't aware of it. I knew he loved airplanes and knew a ton about them, so I made him a plane-themed reminder sign.

I found a basic black image of an airplane online, brought it into PowerPoint, and put a thick vertical line just below the plane to portray a runway. I made two pictures side by side: one showed the plane still in the air coming in for a landing, the other showed the plane landing on the runway. Above the images, I typed in bold: "Land Your Letters on the Runway."

Printed it. Laminated it.

I kept it small, as I do all these sorts of signs and cue cards. It was about the size of a large postcard.

When I presented it to him, his smile was

Land Your Letters on the Runway

priceless. He asked to keep this at his desk, which gave me a simple way to remind him about it before and during writing projects. Because the target behavior happened at specific times, I suggested he keep it in his pencil case, which was easily accessible but also appropriate since he'd be using it during writing times, and it would be easy to grab a pencil and the little sign at the same time.

Now, instead of saying "Remember to write neatly," which he'd probably heard hundreds of times in his life and had tuned out, I said, "Land 'em on the runway!" Or I just made my hand into an airplane and lowered it toward the tabletop to remind him. It always made him smile, and he knew exactly what I was talking about. Better yet, because this was his high-interest topic, it made it fun for him to try to write neater.

It took a few weeks, but with consistent use of the chart and verbal support, he was able to land his letters safely on the runway. Eventually, the sign took a backseat, no longer being taken out at writing times. He was landing his letters on the line naturally, and what's more, he had developed some self-awareness of his challenge with neatness.

This little sign was targeting a very specific issue for Oscar, and I used a very specific interest of his to engage him. With the airplane sign, I happened to find a perfect metaphor for the skill that also matched his interest, and that doesn't always happen, but you might be surprised at what you can come up with for your students. Let's say your student really likes football. Instead of a runway, you can make the lines into sidelines of a football field and write, "Don't go out of bounds!" If a student is interested in fantasy like *The Lord of the Rings* or *Harry Potter,* you could put a wizard on there, saying "Stay on the path, young Hobbit." For a student who's into pop music, how about a picture of Bruno Mars on a straight line: "Keep Bruno on the dance floor."

You get the idea. It's actually fun trying to come up with these connections.

You don't have to have the perfect metaphor for every sign you make, but incorporating a student's interest isn't difficult. Usually the mere image of the interest—whether it be a specific character, a sports team logo, or a favorite emoji—draws their attention to the card, leaving you free to clearly represent the quality-check skill despite it not connecting thematically.

Editing our own writing is another area where we check the quality of our work. For students who are producing writing consistently, the next step is for them to take over editing responsibilities. This is especially difficult for students with attention challenges because they have spent a lot of mental energy on producing a draft, and they may have little left over for proofreading their work.

Here, too, a visual cue can be just the right tool.

ATTENTION GRABBER
The Editing Is Baked Right In

Benjamin, my student who struggled with editing his work, was good at baking delicious confections at home; he would often bring in brownies to share with teachers and classmates. Keeping this interest in mind, I designed an editing checklist for him that connected baking ingredients and writing ingredients.

This sign was a full page. The bottom half consisted of two columns listing the standard writing conventions such as punctuation, capitalization, and spelling, along with transition words, main idea sentence, and a few others. Next to each item was a little box to check off. I didn't reinvent the wheel here—pretty standard for an editing checklist.

What made the checklist different was the top of the sheet—I put a picture of a glorious cake and a picture of typical baking ingredients. Above the images was the phrase, "If you want the cake to come out like this, check your ingredients!" Adding this little baking touch to the checklist helped connect Benjamin to it and, consequently, to the editing itself.

Writing is like BAKING

If you want your *cake* to come out like this . . .

. . . you need all the right ingredients!

WRITING INGREDIENTS

- ○ **Capitals** and **punctuation** (. , ! ?)
- ○ **Indent** at the beginning of paragraphs
- ○ **Transition** words
  (First, Next, Then, After that, Finally, And, Also)
- ○ **Descriptive** words
- ○ **Neat** letters and words
- ○ Correct **spelling**
- ○ **Main idea** sentence
- ○ **Detail** sentences

Whenever writing projects were assigned, Benjamin took out the chart as he was writing to remind himself about conventions. When he completed his rough draft, he went through the checklist to make sure he included everything.

Soon enough, other students took notice of the checklist and were asking for a copy to keep at their desks, and we integrated this tool into the writing process for the whole class. Benjamin was proud that it was his chart first.

Again, you could probably relate any student's interest to the concept of a list. Your student loves a certain pop star? How about, "Make sure your writing plays all these hits!" The student likes horses? Make the boxes into hoof prints and write, "Groom your writing like you would a horse!"

Okay, that one's a stretch.

But it doesn't really matter. What does matter is that the visual cue draws the student's interest and makes it fun while the checklist itself helps build self-awareness.

Mental Energy

Our students' mental energy levels can be inconsistent. Sometimes they're ready to go, listening and working. Other times, not so much. Also, whether they got enough sleep the night before or whether they had a good breakfast can be highly influential factors in whether they're able to focus and participate in your classroom on any given day. It is always important to consider these possibilities when you see students operating much slower than usual, because it helps us better determine how to assist them.

But getting students to be aware of their own swings in energy— that is, to realize when their mental energy is up, when it's low, or when their mind is overactive and they can't sustain one line of thought—is key to helping them respond to their own mental states with the appropriate actions. If someone is mentally exhausted, that person shouldn't be continuing to grind away at work; take a break! If someone's mind is racing too fast, she or he might need a break, too, but of a different sort—a moment to calm down. If they skipped breakfast, maybe they just need five minutes to eat a bit of their snack.

"Mental Energy" Gauge

Younger students often don't articulate that they're tired or over-heated. To help them self-reflect, you can make a "Mental Energy" gauge, a simple visual cue that helps students express how their mental energy is feeling at the moment. The idea is to give three or four choices for students to pick from in determining how they're feeling, ranging from low mental energy to feeling overly excited.

First, think of a theme that could represent energy levels, one that will suit the student's interests. It might be a rocket ship for a kid who's into space or science, a dog or lion for animal lovers, or a basketball player for sports fans. On the back (unlined side) of an index card—no bigger than four by six inches—place three or four images of that object or figure in different phases of motion. You can draw them yourself or pull images from the web. For your low energy spot, pick something like a dog sleeping or an exhausted NFL player on the sidelines. For the steady energy spot in the middle, choose an image showing some basic motion: a person swimming, a skateboarder doing a trick, a horse mid-stride, and so forth. Last, put an image that shows something overheating or looking manic, like an angry cat about to pounce or a water balloon bursting. Label the sections "Low Energy," "Steady Energy" and "Overheated!" or whatever words you think the student will under-stand. Laminate the card, punch a hole in the bottom center, and put a brass fastener through it, bending the arms so it creates a pointer.

Mental Energy

Introduce the gauge to your students by showing them that depending on their mental energy level, the dial can point to any of the "Energy" sections. For younger students, you can act out how someone looks at each level and have them act it out too.

Set designated times when students should check in with their mental energy gauge, such as just before independent work time or other specific times when you think they may need it. Tell them they can also check in with themselves about their own mental energy and let you know how they're doing. Certainly, if you notice a student exhibiting impulsive behaviors and acting a bit manically, that would be a good time to have the student sit down and check in with himself using the gauge.

Just making themselves conscious of their energy levels can be valuable, but students also can make adjustments when it's necessary. If students are low on energy, empower them to try filling their own mental energy tank by grabbing a quick snack outside the room or doing a few laps to regulate their energy level. If they're running overheated, maybe a walk and drink of water will do the trick.

I've even made a gauge like this for use with an entire classroom but with a slightly different goal. A co-teacher was describing for me how the energy in her class would often grow rapidly at times, to the point where kids were calling out constantly and taking over the room, so to speak. I made a gauge using weather as a metaphor. A nice, sunny day was on the left, some storm clouds forming in the middle, and on the right, a full on thunderstorm. The teacher put this on the board, stuck some Velcro on the three spots, and made a little token that stood for the class. The goal was for the class to remain on the sunny day, showing them that their energy level was just right for optimal learning—students are attentive, raising their hands, remaining calm. When a few students began to call out and a lot of off-topic side-conversations were happening, the teacher moved the token to the middle to show that the energy level was rising a bit, with storm clouds forming. If the energy rose even further, with students raising their voices or arguing with each other or talking back to her, she'd move the token to the thunderstorm.

The teacher would move the token between the three weather patterns as the classroom changed its energy level as a whole, and the students would usually respond by taking their energy down a notch. The gauge worked better than trying to yell over them. I have since used this sign in classrooms with a similar issue and have seen the impact it can have in making the class as a whole aware of its own energy levels.

GUEST SPEAKER
MARCIE GILBERT

Marcie Gilbert started her career in education as a classroom teacher and currently works as an educational therapist. Her master's thesis was related to social-emotional learning (SEL), and for years she has implemented programs in schools to foster students' self-awareness and metacognition.

SEL is a broad discipline whose aims include improving students' mindfulness, listening skills, and perspective taking. Viable research shows that even simple SEL exercises can build self-awareness, which results in strengthening executive functions.

Building self-awareness might start with noticing one's senses and surroundings, so here's a short, simple technique I've used in school settings with students with various types of learning and emotional challenges. Once students know the routine, this exercise lasts a minute or so, which makes it easy to integrate at the beginning of class or after breaks.

The exercise starts with turning off the lights and asking students to close their eyes. I start with sound, and with each sense, I might instruct students to count how many of a thing they can detect or guide them to a particular one: for example, "If you hear cars driving by, touch your nose."

Next, I ask students to focus on their sense of smell. You can also use these moments to build students' vocabularies. For instance, does the room smell *musty*, like an old couch, or *pungent*, like cleaning products?

Taste is next: "Can you still taste your lunch? Was it sweet? Spicy? Does your mouth taste stale, like you could go for a piece of gum?"

Last, I have them notice their hands and what they're touching, including texture and temperature. I guide them to touch thumb to pinky, thumb to ring finger, thumb to middle finger, and thumb to pointer finger while focusing on the feeling of their fingers touching.

If there's time at the end of the exercise, with their eyes still closed, I ask students to choose one word to describe their emotional state. When students open their eyes, we quickly circle around the classroom and share our words. This can be furthered to having students think metaphorically. For example, students might provide a "weather report" for how they're feeling: "sunny" for happy, "windy" for restless, and so on. Older students can handle more sophisticated analogies, such as hashtags, songs, TV shows, or food (like "soggy fries" for feeling sluggish).

Inevitably, some students will act silly until the activity becomes something they're accustomed to. Most students with whom I've conducted this exercise come from families or neighborhoods where self-reflection is not part of their family or community culture. Anticipating potential silliness, I frontload students with information and expectations regarding what we'll be doing, and I don't fight against it when it happens. Normally, after the activity becomes familiar, the silliness goes away.

Once students are accustomed to the exercise, I phase out verbal scaffolding so that they are simply quiet and being directed to notice sounds, scents, tastes, and sensations in/on their hands.

As a means to calm or ground themselves whenever needed, students can pull out a piece of the exercise and use it at other times, such as touching their thumb to each finger underneath their desks or closing their eyes and focusing on one sense. Consequently, this is a strategy that students can generalize to any given moment in their lives, whether they're experiencing anxiety or needing focus.

Marcie describes a totally different approach to building self-awareness, and I believe it's one that should and will be explored more commonly in our classrooms in the coming years. In this frenetic world we live in, it can be calming to stop for a moment and recognize what we're currently feeling and how we are responding to our environment.

This applies even more profoundly to our students with attention challenges. Imagine how beneficial it could be for a student who is feeling overwhelmed, anxious, or drained of mental energy to be able to self-assess and then articulate those feelings to a teacher, friend, or even just to herself or himself.

The routine Marcie describes isn't complicated. Any teacher can lead students in a guided meditation like this, and it doesn't take very long. What an effective way to reintegrate your students to the classroom after lunch and help build self-awareness muscles in the process.

Time Management and Production

Time management can be tough for all of us, especially in the internet age. It is incredibly easy, for example, to waste away time going down the rabbit holes of pop culture on YouTube. One minute you're checking your email, about to get started on that work project due tomorrow, then before you know it, you're on your sixth "Weird Al" Yankovic video, the sun has gone down, and the project is still due tomorrow!

I speak from experience, clearly.

Being able to schedule our time and figure out how much time tasks require is at the base of being able to get things done and reach short-term goals.

This is a tough one for some students. Students with production issues often take a lot of time to complete or even just start assignments. Or they may spend too long on a given question or focus too much energy on one aspect of an assignment. That's on top of the consistent distraction they experience that breaks up their productivity. And with technology so readily accessible, it makes these sorts of self-management skills even more challenging. Imagine if we saw an accurate figure of how much time we fritter away online or on other technologies . . . yikes.

We can help bring time awareness to our students with the use of timers. Timers can be used during independent work to help students balance working and break times, and also grow their awareness about how they spend their time—and how they can manage it more effectively, so they get the most out of their mental energy.

You may notice students who work diligently for a period of time and then maybe take a quick break—stop for a minute to sharpen a pencil, walk across the room, or just stretch out their arms—and then they get back to work. They innately understand that they need to take short breaks to recharge their mental energy, and then they return to their business.

Students with time management difficulties can't assess these sorts of time increments. Whether I'm teaching in a classroom or in one-to-one settings, students often ask me, "What time is it?" or

"How much time is left?" or even "How long have we been working?" These questions are an easy transition into growing their self-awareness, and the next step is simple as well:

Use actual timers for individual students who struggle with time management. You can also use them with your whole class, if you think everyone would benefit.

I use timers frequently with some of my students in one-to-one sessions. These are students who need breaks, so their cognitive muscles can relax for a bit while their mental energy reloads. When students are in the middle of a work time but drained of mental energy, they'll probably just sit there idle, stressed about the tasks in front of them. It's important they take a brain break to allow their minds to rest while they move around, get a quick drink, and get the blood circulating so they'll be ready for round two.

But how long should their break be? This is something I talk to my students about. "How long of a break should we take?" I ask.

"Ten minutes," one might say.

"Hmm . . . well, that's a large chunk of time. Usually when we eat a meal, it takes about ten or fifteen minutes . . . and we don't want to lose too much of the time we have to work on this. Do you think five might do the trick?"

"Yeah, five would work."

Engaging students in this discussion helps them develop an awareness of time increments in relation to getting work done. In your classroom, you could have this conversation with your students as a group and set a timer accordingly. This can include you saying something like, "All right, we're going to work on our essays for ten minutes and then take a five-minute break," a cue for students to start exerting some brain power knowing that a break is on the horizon. I like to introduce timers by setting them myself, and after a few times, I let students do it to help build their sense of responsibility.

You can use a kitchen timer or a little plastic digital timer, which you can pick up for three to ten dollars online or at a home goods or department store. There are also apps you can get on your phone like Time Timer, which shows time ticking down in a highly visible way, and of course, there's always your phone's built-in clock app.

Using a timer is not always beneficial. Many of our students with learning challenges receive accommodations in the form of extra time for work, quizzes, and tests, which can be crucial to their being able to complete the work to the best of their abilities. It may be that for these students, using a timer adds pressure and ends up being counterproductive to the purpose of the accommodations. Be attentive to how timers affect your students. If the presence of the timer adds pressure to a student, causing her to feel stressed, rush through an assignment, and produce careless work, the timer is probably doing more harm than good.

In this case, you could try setting the timer away from the students and monitoring it and reminding them occasionally about the timer. If it's out of their immediate sight, they may not feel as pressured by it while still having a general awareness of the time allotted for the task and their own time spent working.

Timers can also be beneficial for students while doing homework. You could lend them your cheap timer to use at home or recommend this strategy to their parents. The goal is for students to set goals for themselves: "I'll spend fifteen minutes reading *Of Mice and Men,* but then I get ten minutes to send some texts and scan through social media. Then I'll work on math for twenty minutes."

Planning Ahead

As students get older, the number of steps required to complete projects increases. There may be a book or textbook chapter to read beforehand. Then there's the brainstorming phase. Next, students may create some sort of outline or planning sheet and then there is the gathering of materials, if necessary. After that, a rough draft or mock-up of the project, some editing, and last, a final draft.

Students with attention deficits usually don't think in these terms. Their modus operandi might be to skip the early steps and rush to the final draft. Perhaps they don't understand that the project contains smaller tasks within it. Maybe it's because the project feels too daunting already, and they'd rather get it over with as quickly as possible. Or, another possibility which happens frequently, they wait until the very last minute to even start, so they skip steps that seem like they will take unnecessary extra time.

In general, it's difficult for these students to assess how much work a project or task is going to take, especially considering their lack of self-awareness about their own behavior. Our affected students need something visual and tangible to help them plan. Going through multistep projects takes patience, planning, and organization. A simple "Step Chart" tool can help slow them down and show them how to break up the project into smaller tasks. Project guidelines usually only break up projects into the main pieces, such as rough draft and final project. With step charts, we can break up the planning into increments as small and numerous as we want.

For students who can't get started because it simply feels too overwhelming, step charts help them see the project as a series of smaller incremental tasks that they will complete over time, relieving the anxiety of having to do it all at once. Due dates can also be placed alongside each step to give students an idea of how much time they have before having to complete the next step.

ATTENTION GRABBER
Small Steps on the Moon for Humankind

Nia, an eighth-grade student, was tasked with writing a short story for her class. I was working with her at school primarily on writing production and learned that she could brainstorm all sorts of interesting concepts, but only when given a specific idea to start with. This assignment happened to be completely open ended; the story could be about anything she chose. Immediately, this was overwhelming to her. The sheer number of possibilities made it difficult for her to even come up with one idea. I made suggestions based on her interests, but she shrugged off all of them. Finally, we did some searching online to help get inspiration and ultimately arrived on an image of space and the moon that she selected as the setting. Okay, step one completed.

Seeing how long it took for her to arrive at just a topic for this story—and recognizing how daunted she was about the project—I made her a step chart so she could see the project in smaller steps. The assignment tasked the students with making a rough draft, a final draft, and a revision, but I designed this step chart to break the project into much smaller and more manageable tasks.

I listed the steps as follows:

1. Brainstorm characters and basic plot

2. Brainstorm into a beginning/middle/end map

3. Edit/add to the map

4. Write opening sentence of story

5. Write beginning of story

6. Write middle of story

7. Write end of story

8. Edit/add extra ideas

9. Edit grammar and spelling

Next to each step, I put boxes so she could check off the steps as she accomplished them throughout the process.

For her, writing a story was a gigantic task. She had many creative thoughts and ideas for her space story once she landed on that topic, but she needed to work through this project slowly, step by step, in order to feel confident with it and produce further. So she brainstormed ideas into a story map, coming up with characters and plot details, which took a few sessions. Once this was completed, she checked off box one. Next, she spent a session putting plot details into a beginning/middle/end chart. Then she edited it and added some more ideas to make sure she had a solid plan for the actual writing—and she checked off steps two and three. I knew landing on an opening sentence would be challenging, so I made that its own step, but she ended up writing a few sentences to start the story before checking off that step.

Having already brainstormed so many ideas into the story map, writing the actual story became a lot easier. And by this time, she was getting in the rhythm of seeing this project in incremental steps instead of as one huge task. In one session, she tackled the beginning, in the next session she wrote the middle, and finally, the end. A session to edit and add ideas to the whole story, and then a session to edit for grammar and spelling, and the step chart was complete—along with her space story. By the way, her story was wholly original, funny, and imaginative, involving an excavation on the moon!

Any sort of project in any subject can be broken up into smaller steps. A project that requires building or making something—maybe a solar system model using Styrofoam balls or a miniature catapult out of popsicle sticks and rubber bands—could be broken up into brainstorming ideas for the project, sketching out a visual of the project, brainstorming materials needed, acquiring materials, construction, and then beautifying as a final step. If the assignment is to make a poster that includes research and experiments, such as for a science fair, the project could be broken up into brainstorming, forming a hypothesis, gathering resources, reading the resources and highlighting key information, deciding on an experiment, gathering materials, conducting the experiment, and designing the poster.

After you introduce step charts to students and show them how to use them by taking them through the process, you can—for ensuing projects—just give them charts to check off the steps on their own. The goal is that they eventually gain an internalization of the process, so they learn to see bigger projects in terms of smaller, incremental steps they can plan and accomplish piece by piece.

Organization of Materials

Oh, the chaos one might find inside a student's desk, backpack, or work binder. Generally, students with messy workspaces, backpacks, and belongings don't appear to know or care about this. They march on, frequently having difficulty locating things or losing things, even objects precious to them. They only clean and organize when called upon to do it, not even to throw away junk or fit paper or pencils neatly in their containers.

Eventually, we all need to take responsibility for our things, but just telling students over and over again to be organized and keep things clean doesn't work for the long term. Instead, you can get students engaged with the organization process with a visual cue.

Help students internalize what it looks like to have things organized. One way to do this—after helping them clean up their desk, backpack, or binder—is to snap a picture. Print it out and give it to students to store in their desks or backpacks or somewhere near the disaster area in question so they have a visual reference of what organization looks like. You could include a check-off chart on the side of the picture with specific organizational details—for example, keeping a desk organized might include keeping pencils and erasers in a case, putting loose papers in a folder, and throwing away any scraps. Students can monitor the situation daily and put a check next to each detail on the chart if the area resembles the picture. If you laminate the picture or put it in a plastic sleeve, students can use dry erase markers and reuse the chart daily.

It's important that these charts are kept near the "area of hazard." If it's a backpack issue, the card could be small and attached to a zipper, perhaps. If it's for the desk, keep it visible on the corner of the desk or propped up inside.

This is going to sound extremely basic and obvious, but sometimes a student just needs the proper container for something. It could be a small plastic box, baggy, binder, or folder, as long as it engages them.

☑ Pencils in case
☑ Papers in folders
☑ Books closed and stacked
☑ Trash and scraps thrown away

<hr>

ATTENTION GRABBER
Cat Got Your Math?
Sometimes all it takes is a small support to help a student get organized. Trey, a fifth grader I worked with after school, had an affinity for felines that I happened to share. At the start of sessions, he'd want to

show me the latest ridiculous cat videos he'd seen, and I would show him pictures of my own cats in various stages of relaxation. Math, on the other hand? He was not such a fan. It seemed like he was forgetting to bring home his math packet every other day, and when he did have it with him, he would wrench it from his backpack all creased and wrinkled like a worn sock to throw in the laundry.

The obvious solution was to get him a folder, but I also felt like associating the packet with something positive might help him engage with the organization process. So I got a packet of folders with cats on them and let him choose one to use for math. He smiled, picked the one with the coolest-looking creature, and from that moment on, when it was time to take out his math packet, I said, "Okay, where's the cat folder?"

I knew he'd be into it, but I wasn't quite expecting how effective the folder was in prompting him to take care of his packets. He rarely misplaced a packet after that.

The Big Takeaway

Students will not always have us to hold up a mirror for them. At some point, they will be on their own, out in the world. They won't have teachers or parents helping them organize their things, reminding them not to interrupt others who are talking, or scheduling their work projects so they meet deadlines. The more self-aware students become regarding the areas in which they struggle, the better equipped they will be to support themselves.

Visual cue cards can remind students of proper behavior like hand raising and maintaining personal space. Step charts can give them the opportunity to literally check off steps in a longer project and internalize the process of breaking larger tasks into smaller steps. Energy gauges can teach students to self-assess their own mental energy levels at a given moment and act accordingly. Guided mindfulness activities can help students get attuned to their senses and surroundings. The goal is that eventually, students internalize the self-awareness so that charts and timers and reminders become unnecessary. Their self-monitoring becomes something they do naturally and consistently throughout the day.

We can start by adjusting those mirrors for students and then handing off the mirror to them, so they can check in with their own behavior.

One step closer to student independence.

Some Chocolate Chips for the Road

Back in chapter 1, I compared including students' interests in your lessons to adding chocolate chips to your cereal. That's how I see this whole book. We're just sprinkling chocolate chips around our classroom and into assignments throughout the day. Not only is it easy, but more importantly, it makes everything just a bit sweeter to make the meal go down easier. That is, it makes the learning and projects more appealing and accessible so your students with attention challenges become more engaged. Maybe it's incorporating fidgets or acting out subtraction problems, discussing how *Black Panther* is Shakespearean, letting a student build a model for a science project instead of writing a paper, or using a baking-themed editing checklist. We can use these tools every day, and the more we use them, the more natural they become—until we're using tools of engagement without any planning at all. They just become part of the routine.

For a teacher of any kind, nothing compares to seeing a struggling student gaining confidence and accomplishing things, no matter how small. Each victory builds on the last, and as they gain momentum, these students begin to see school as a place that offers them opportunities to feel successful.

Our work in this area is not just about helping students achieve in terms of tests and grades. It's about growing their engagement in a broader sense. It's about helping them feel valuable, not just as students but as people. They're learning about what interests them and what they have to offer. They're figuring out how they fit into social groups and how they function in formal settings like classrooms.

No one wants to feel overwhelmed, anxious, or incapable of participating and succeeding. Students want to feel confident, to feel like their interests matter, and to feel like they can achieve. Though sometimes it may not seem like it, students *want* to be engaged.

Our students with challenges are often at risk of feeling beaten down or defeated by school. When we create an environment where they feel confident enough to share their interests and talents with us, where they know they can make mistakes and that's okay, where they believe their ideas and skills are valued, and where they can experience success, they don't simply increase their engagement. They start to feel capable and important.

When that happens . . . the world is their chocolate chip cookie.

NOTES

1. ADDitude. "ADHD, By the Numbers." www.additudemag.com/the-statistics-of-adhd.

2. ADDitude. "ADHD, By the Numbers." www.additudemag.com/the-statistics-of-adhd.

3. Bouffard, Thérèse, et al. "Changes in Self-Perceptions of Competence and Intrinsic Motivation Among Elementary Schoolchildren." *British Journal of Educational Psychology* 73, no. 2 (2003): 171–186, doi: 10.1348/00070990360626921.

4. Fedewa, Alicia L., and Heather E. Erwin. "Stability Balls and Students with Attention and Hyperactivity Concerns: Implications for On-Task and In-Seat Behavior." *American Journal of Occupational Therapy* 65 (2011): 393–399, doi: 10.5014/ajot2011.000554.

5. Best, John R. "Effects of Physical Activity on Children's Executive Function: Contributions of Experimental Research on Aerobic Exercise." *Developmental Review* 30, no. 4 (2010): 331–551.

6. Trilling, Bernie, and Charles Fadel. *21st Century Skills: Learning for Life in Our Times.* Jossey-Bass, 2012.

7. MacArthur, Charles A. "Reflections on Research on Writing and Technology for Struggling Writers." *Learning Disabilities Research & Practice* 24, no. 2 (2009): 93–103, doi:10.1111/j.1540-5826.2009.00283.x.

8. Longcamp, Marieke, et al. "The Influence of Writing Practice on Letter Recognition in Preschool Children: A Comparison Between Handwriting and Typing." *Acta Psychologica* 119, no. 1 (2005): 67–79, doi:10.1016/j.actpsy.2004.10.019.

9. Wolfson, Gene. "Using Audiobooks to Meet the Needs of Adolescent Readers." *American Secondary Education* 36, no. 2 (2008): 105–114.

Books

American Psychiatric Association. *Diagnostic and Statistical Manual of Mental Disorders, Fifth Edition.* American Psychiatric Publishing, 2013.

Bear, Donald R., et al. *Words Their Way: Word Study for Phonics, Vocabulary, and Spelling Instruction.* Pearson, 2015.

Ficksman, Maxine, and Jane Utley Adelizzi (eds). *The Clinical Practice of Educational Therapy: Learning and Functioning with Diversity.* Routledge, 2018.

Hallowell, Edward M., and John J Ratey. *Driven to Distraction: Recognizing and Coping with Attention Deficit Disorder from Childhood Through Adulthood.* Random House, Inc., 2011.

Minskoff, Esther. *Teaching Reading to Struggling Learners.* Paul H. Brookes Publishing Co., 2005.

Rothschild, Melanie. *The Art of Mistakes: Unexpected Painting Techniques & the Practice of Creative Thinking.* North Light Books, 2014.

Trilling, Bernie, and Charles Fadel. *21st Century Skills: Learning for Life in Our Times.* Jossey-Bass, 2012.

Articles

Best, John R. "Effects of Physical Activity on Children's Executive Function: Contributions of Experimental Research on Aerobic Exercise." *Developmental Review* 30, no. 4 (2010): 331–551.

Bouffard, Thérèse, et al. "Changes in Self-Perceptions of Competence and Intrinsic Motivation Among Elementary Schoolchildren." *British Journal of Educational Psychology* 73, no. 2 (2003): 171–186, doi: 10.1348/00070990360626921.

Brooks, Robert. "The Search for Islands of Competence: A Metaphor of Hope and Strength." June 17, 2005. www.drrobertbrooks.com/0506.

Englert, Carol Sue, et al. "Scaffolding the Writing of Students with Disabilities Through Procedural Facilitation Using an Internet-Based Technology to Improve Performance." *Learning Disability Quarterly* 30, no. 1 (2007): 9–29.

Fedewa, Alicia L., and Heather E. Erwin. "Stability Balls and Students with Attention and Hyperactivity Concerns: Implications for On-Task and In-Seat Behavior." *American Journal of Occupational Therapy* 65 (2011): 393–399, doi: 10.5014/ajot2011.000554.

Gonzalez, Michelle. "The Effect of Embedded Text-to-Speech and Vocabulary eBook Scaffolds on the Comprehension of Students with Reading Disabilities." *International Journal of Special Education* 29, no. 3 (2014): 111–126.

Larson, Lotta C. "Digital Readers: The Next Chapter in E-Book Reading and Response." *The Reading Teacher* 64, no. 1 (2010): 15–22, doi: 10.1598/RT.64.1.2.

Longcamp, Marieke, et al. "The Influence of Writing Practice on Letter Recognition in Preschool Children: A Comparison Between Handwriting and Typing." *Acta Psychologica* 119, no. 1 (2005): 67–79, doi:10.1016/j.actpsy.2004.10.019.

MacArthur, Charles A. "Reflections on Research on Writing and Technology for Struggling Writers." *Learning Disabilities Research & Practice* 24, no. 2 (2009): 93–103, doi:10.1111/j.1540-5826.2009.00283.x.

Office of Educational Technology. "Reimagining the Role of Technology in Education: 2017 National Education Technology Plan Update." January 2017. tech.ed.gov/files/2017/01/NETP17.pdf.

Wolfson, Gene. "Using Audiobooks to Meet the Needs of Adolescent Readers." *American Secondary Education* 36, no. 2 (2008): 105–114.

Websites, Organizations, and Other Resources

ADDitude Magazine
www.additudemag.com

BrainPOP (animated educational resources)
www.brainpop.com

CHADD: Children and Adults with Attention-Deficit/Hyperactivity Disorder—The National Resource on ADHD
www.chadd.org

CrashCourse (educational YouTube channel)
www.youtube.com/user/crashcourse

Dance Mat Typing (free typing practice)
www.dancemattypingguide.com

Goodreads: Graphic Novel Adaptations of Classic Books
www.goodreads.com/list/show/34639.Graphic_Novel_Adaptations_of_Classic_Books

MyON (reading and instructional content)
www.myon.com/index.html

Newsela (reading and instructional content)
newsela.com

Shmoop (teacher and literature resources)
www.shmoop.com

TED-Ed (videos for teachers to develop lessons)
ed.ted.com

INDEX

Ezra Werb, M.Ed., formerly a behavior interventionist and resource specialist teacher and currently an educational therapist, has been working with students with attention deficits, learning challenges, and spectrum disorders in typical classroom settings, resource rooms, and one-on-one academic support scenarios for more than a dozen years. Ezra earned his master's in special education with a concentration in educational therapy from Cal-State Northridge and is a member of the Association of Educational Therapists. He lives in Los Angeles, California, where he works in private practice with students with ADHD, spectrum disorders, dyslexia, anxiety, and other learning challenges.

Other Great Resources from Free Spirit

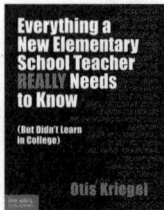

Everything a New Elementary School Teacher REALLY Needs to Know
(But Didn't Learn in College)
by Otis Kriegel
For new elementary teachers, preservice teachers, and administrators.
224 pp.; PB; 6" x 7½".

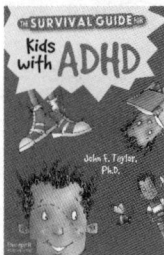

Self-Regulation in the Classroom
Helping Students Learn How to Learn
by Richard M. Cash, Ed.D.
For K–12 teachers, administrators, and counselors.
184 pp.; PB; 8½" x 11"; includes digital content.
Free PLC/Book Study Guide
freespirit.com/PLC

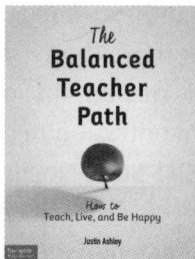

The Survival Guide for Kids with ADHD
(Updated Edition)
by John F. Taylor, Ph.D.
For ages 8–12.
128 pp.; PB; two-color; illust.; 6" x 9".

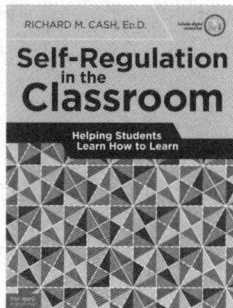

The Balanced Teacher Path
How to Teach, Live, and Be Happy
by Justin Ashley
For educators, grades K–8.
160 pp.; PB; 7¼" x 9¼".

Interested in purchasing multiple quantities and receiving volume discounts?
Contact edsales@freespirit.com or call 1.800.735.7323 and ask for Education Sales.

Many Free Spirit authors are available for speaking engagements, workshops, and keynotes. Contact speakers@freespirit.com or call 1.800.735.7323.

For pricing information, to place an order, or to request a free catalog, contact:

Free Spirit Publishing Inc. • 6325 Sandburg Road, Suite 100 • Minneapolis, MN 55427-3674
toll-free 800.735.7323 • local 612.338.2068 • fax 612.337.5050
help4kids@freespirit.com • www.freespirit.com